A Companion Workbook
of
Spiritual Exercises
for
What's Your God Language?

by
Dr. Myra Perrine

ISBN-10: 1508669651
ISBN-13: 978-1508669654

Dedication

This book is for all those who hunger for
Christ to dwell in their hearts by faith, so that they,
being rooted and established in love, may have power,
together with all the saints, to grasp how wide and long and high and deep
is the love of Christ, and to know this love that surpasses knowledge—
that they may be filled to the measure of all the fullness of God.

And to Him who is able to do immeasurably more than all we can ask or
imagine, according to His power that is at work within us.
(Ephesians 3:17-20).

Table of Contents

Acknowledgements

Many thanks to my friends at Tyndale House Publishers.
All I can say is, WOW!
Sharon Leavitt, you have become like family to me.
Jan Long Harris, your generosity is overwhelming.
Who knew nearly a decade ago that we'd still be
journeying together all these years later?
What a gift the Tyndale family is to me,
and I appreciate you greatly!

Introduction

Welcome to the Companion Workbook of Spiritual Exercises designed to accompany, *What's Your God Language? Connecting with God Through Your Unique Spiritual Temperament.*

In *What's Your God Language? (WYGL?)*, we learned that each follower of Christ has a unique spiritual temperament—our way of knowing and loving God. And though our spiritual temperaments reveal our spiritual *preferences* (how we *most naturally* come to God), when our preferences align with corresponding spiritual *practices* (how we *more deliberately* come to God), greater passion for Jesus can result!

The Intermediate and Advanced Exercises

WYGL? introduced nine spiritual temperament categories, along with Beginning Spiritual Practice Exercises for each one. This Companion Workbook is for those who want to keep growing beyond the beginning exercises; it offers six more weeks of INTERMEDIATE and ADVANCED Spiritual Exercises for all nine spiritual temperaments. Each chapter—arranged alphabetically from the Activist to the Traditionalist—highlights one spiritual temperament, and every section is divided into three weeklong practices to be utilized based on the results of your Spiritual Temperament Inventory found in Chapter 2 of *WYGL?*

Begin by selecting the exercises that correspond with your most *passionate* spiritual temperaments—those that are strongest and most readily stir your passion for God, and where you scored *highest* on your Spiritual Temperament Inventory. Then proceed through the workbook to your *pleasurable* spiritual temperaments—those you enjoy that nurture your love for God, and where you scored in the *moderate* range. Conclude with your *potential* spiritual temperaments—those that are relatively unused and undeveloped, and where you scored the *lowest*.

Let me say before you begin that some of the Intermediate and Advanced Exercises are designed to be a stretch for you and invite you out of your comfort zone. That's because these exercises are intended to help you grow in your most passionate as well as your least developed spiritual temperaments. As was stated in *WYGL?* the research I gathered during my doctoral project showed that when people were exposed to spiritual practices across all nine spiritual temperaments, they reported being more "hungry" for God. In other words, the more experience people had connecting with God in a variety of ways—even those outside their preferences—the stronger their desire for Jesus tended to be (for more information on this, see the Introduction in *WYGL?* which discusses my findings after interviewing more than seventy ministry leaders). Thus, as you continue on with these practices, you will likely grow in new ways and see your appetite for the Lord increase. That being said, if you find yourself NOT wanting to do some of the exercises, I encourage you to push through and keep going, realizing that spiritual fruit *will come*—sometimes right away, sometimes later.

Our Part and God's Part

In spiritual formation, repetition is one way God's Spirit meets us at ever-deepening levels, making us more like Jesus. Therefore, each week we will focus on only one exercise, giving ample opportunity for you to proceed at the pace that works best for you, revisiting the activity as many times as you'd like during the week. Feel free to take as much or as little time as you need for each exercise. Remember that our life with God is an ongoing love relationship—a process and a lifelong journey with *a Person*. Therefore, finishing these exercises is not the goal; knowing and loving Jesus is! These activities simply provide a place for you to meet the Holy Spirit and spend authentic time together, progressively opening your heart to His transformative presence. I encourage you to avoid letting the structure of these exercises bog you down, but give the Lord room to take you where He will. Listen for His voice and notice how and where His Spirit is bringing life, for He promises to be the Rewarder of those who diligently seek Him (see Hebrews 11:6). As Sam Metcalf, the President of Church Resource Ministries, says:

> The older I get, the more I realize that God is remarkably accommodating, far beyond my imagination or comprehension. He so longs to relate with me that He will go to great extremes to overcome the frailties of my humanity. Consider what He has done throughout redemptive history and the huge variety of means He has employed to reveal Himself: angels, a pillar of fire, a Temple, an ass, an audible voice from heaven. . . . Like all liturgical practice, regularity [of time with God] can bring confidence and surety [with Him]. It is like the regular exercise of a muscle. However, while discipline is certainly admirable, structure without grace can be the death of real spiritual vitality.[1]

Yes, this workbook offers some structure, but it is only the grace of God that surrounds us, enfolds us, and changes us; it's His grace that gives us life. Isn't it wonderful to know that when all is said and done, our transformation into the image of Christ is God's work, and nothing lasting will occur apart from Him? So as you do these exercises, invite—no, *expect!*—God's Spirit to meet you. Ours is a love-relationship that began by grace, and it is grace that leads us on. As Richard Foster says:

> God will not enter many areas of our life uninvited.
> So we invite God to enter every experience of life:
> We invite God to set our spirit free for worship and adoration.
> We invite God to animate our preaching and praying and singing.
> We invite God to heal our bodies.
> We invite God to inform our minds with creative ideas for our business enterprises.
> We invite God to touch broken relationships and resolve conflicts at work or home.
> We invite God to make our homes holy places of worship and study and work and play and lovemaking. We invite . . . we invite.
> Perhaps we could speak of this as "invited grace." [2]

May God's *invited grace* usher you more deeply into His presence—day by day—as you meet our Living Lord in these exercises.

---

[1] This entry appeared on Sam Metcalf's personal blog (January 2007).
[2] I received this as a handout in the Spiritual Foundations class Richard Foster taught in January 2001, at Azusa Pacific University, Azusa, CA.

1

The Activist
Loving God through Confrontation with Evil

Intermediate Spiritual Practices for the Activist

Week 1 ~ The Activist ~

READ: However we connect most naturally with God, the Bible tells all Christ-followers to uphold the cause of those who don't have the political, social, or economic power to care for themselves. We are given the charge to lend our influence to those who are not able to defend themselves, to use our voices justly by standing up for the powerless—those who are not given an opportunity to be heard. Here are passages that state this:

> "Cursed is the man who withholds justice from the alien, the fatherless or the widow" (*Deuteronomy 27:19*).

> "Prove yourselves doers of the word, and not merely hearers who delude themselves. For if anyone is a hearer of the word and not a doer, he is like a man who looks at his natural face in a mirror; for once he has looked at himself and gone away, he has immediately forgotten what kind of person he was. But one who looks intently at the perfect law, the law of liberty, and abides by it, not having become a forgetful hearer but an effectual doer, this man will be blessed in what he does…. Pure and undefiled religion in the sight of our God and Father is this: to visit orphans and widows in their distress, and to keep oneself unstained by the world" (*James 1:22-25, 27, NASB*).

> "God's righteous people will pour themselves out for the poor, but the ungodly make no attempt to understand or help the needy" (*Proverbs 29:7, The Passion Translation*).

REFLECT: Ask God to show you the people in your sphere of influence—family, neighbors, church, or community—who need your advocacy because they do not have the political, social, or economic power to care for themselves: the alien (those who live near you but are not citizens), the fatherless (those who have lost a parent), and the widow (those who have lost a husband or wife due to death, divorce, or desertion). Consider how the Lord is inviting you to get involved or lend your voice, your advocacy, and your strength. Wait on Him today for insight and discernment about who these people might be.

Jot down the names and ideas that come to mind:

RESPOND: Based on what the Lord showed you, ask Him for the grace and wisdom to actively care for one person who came to mind. Then step out and take action this week, depending upon Him to lead.

RECORD: How did the Lord lead you to take action this week?

How did you see or feel Jesus' presence as you stepped out to be an advocate for another?

What follow-up needs to take place?

Share your experience with a friend you can trust, asking him to check in with you next month about this situation and any further action necessary.

Write a prayer now committing your steps to the Lord (see Psalm 37:5).

Week 2 ~ **The Activist** ~

READ: In her book, *Suffering*, Dorothee Soelle says that middle-class society insulates itself from the discomfort of those who are in distress—even from the hurt inside themselves. She states that in our materialist desire for heaven on earth, we anesthetize ourselves against feeling pain of any kind and will only move toward that which is "orderly and therefore unfelt."[3] Yet God allows Himself to feel the pain of others. He is known as the Man of sorrows, the One who is acquainted with grief (see Isaiah 53:3),

REFLECT: Look around your family, neighborhood, church, and community. What are a few of the situations that may be causing pain to the heart of God?

As a Man of sorrows who is acquainted with grief, ask Jesus to show you how you can share in the sorrow and anguish your world is causing Him. Write what comes to mind:

---

[3] Dorothee Soelle, *Suffering* (Philadelphia: Fortress, 1975).

RESPOND: This week step out and walk toward that pain with Jesus. If it means agreeing with Him in prayer, then intercede. If it means moving toward a person in need, do not try to meet her need financially.[4] Instead, ask God for the grace to begin or strengthen a genuine relationship with her so that Jesus can incarnationally (in the flesh) love and serve her through you. Ask for wisdom not to see her as a "project" or person to be "helped", but to relate to her genuinely and lovingly as someone highly cherished by the Lord.[5]

RECORD: How did you take action this week?

How did you see or feel Jesus with you as stepped out?

What follow-up do you need to do now?

Share your experience with a friend you can trust, asking her to check in with you next month about this situation and any further action necessary.

Write a prayer now committing your steps to the Lord (see Psalm 37:5).

---

[4] For ease in reading, I will alternate using "she" or "he" to represent both genders throughout this book.
[5] The book, *When Helping Hurts: Alleviating Poverty Without Hurting the Poor. . .and Yourself,* by Brian Fikkert, explains how faulty assumptions about poverty often cause those who want to help the poor to actually harm them. I recommend this book for those desiring to have an effective, holistic ministry to the poor.

INTEGRATION: Review the last two weeks. What has God taught you and how has He changed your heart?

How will what you have learned become a way of life?

If there is more you still need to do, write it here or in your journal.

Now receive God's grace and reflect upon His unalterable love for you—no matter how well you think you completed these spiritual exercises.

Advanced Spiritual Practices for the Activist

Week 1 ~ **The Activist** ~

READ: Maintaining proper perspective is crucial in any ministry, but is especially important for the serious Activist. As he continually realigns his heart to the heart of God, this not only deepens his impact, but it protects him from burnout and other unforeseen pitfalls that can accompany being highly involved in a cause.

The prophet Micah said, "He has showed you, oh man, what is good. And what does the Lord require of you? To act justly and to love mercy and to walk humbly with your God" *(Micah 6:8).*

REFLECT: In the Lord's economy, acts of justice must be accompanied by mercy, humility, and walking closely with Jesus. Take a few minutes to stop and examine your own heart and character by completing this personal inventory, ranking how you're doing in the following areas. Think deeply about each one and be as honest as you can with yourself *(1 is low; 5 is high):*

_____ Compassion *(sympathy and concern for the suffering of others, with a desire to assist in some way)*

_____ Courage *(the ability to face difficulty, uncertainty, or the threat of pain without retreating or being sidetracked)*

_____ Wisdom *(the insight and experience needed to see life from God's point of view, then applying that in everyday life)*

_____ Knowledge *(attentiveness to facts and an ability to assess data based on God's ways and principles)*

_____ Humility *(a high regard and respect for others with no assumption of superiority, judgment, or self-importance)*

_____ Empathy *(the capacity to sense and feel the pain of others)*

_____ A servant's heart *(the desire to be God's hands and feet to a lost world)*

_____ Grief *(the habit of weeping over your own sin and the sins of others)*

_____ Holiness *(the ability to love the sinner while hating the sin, and remaining close enough to Jesus to avoid the internal and external snares of evils pull)*

_____ Being motivated only by God's glory *(the willingness to listen to people who are different from you, not evaluating them based upon how they can help you or how active they are in your cause)*

_____ Forgiveness *(the ability to bless those who oppose your vision and passion)*

_____ Eternal perspective *(the habit of blessing those who curse you, then moving your eyes back toward God)*

RESPOND: How did you do overall on this personal inventory?

Add up your scores: _____. Then divide by 12:_____. If you scored an average of 4 or 5, you are most likely responding in sync with God's heart as you move to accomplish justice in your area of influence. If your average is 3, you may want to ask the Lord to help you regain His heart and perspective in each area where this was your score. If your score was an average of 1 or 2, you probably need to take a break—time away from your cause to be with

God and rest in Him. Ask the Lord to help you regain His heart-motivation of compassion, as well as His big-picture perspective.

After reflecting on the personal inventory, what changes is the Lord inviting you to make in your life?

In what ways do you need the Father to refresh, heal, or reshape your heart and character to become more like Christ's?

RECORD: In light of your score on the inventory, if you are needing extended rest, what would be most helpful for you?

What follow-up do you need to do now?

Share your experience with a friend you can trust, asking him to check in with you next month about this situation and any further action necessary.

Write a prayer now committing your steps to the Lord (see Psalm 37:5).

Week 2 ~ **The Activist** ~

READ: In *WYGL*, Activists are described as having a tenacious desire to see evil confronted and good prevail, even at great personal expense. In fact, they can often be found in highly challenging environments that push them to the limit of their capacity. In Exodus 18 we see how God helped one Activist survive in ministry:

> "The next day Moses took his seat to serve as judge for the people, and they stood around him from morning till evening. When his father-in-law saw all that Moses was doing for the people, he said, 'What is this you are doing for the people? Why do you alone sit as judge, while all these people stand around you from morning till evening?'

> Moses answered him, 'Because the people come to me to seek God's will. Whenever they have a dispute, it is brought to me, and I decide between the parties and inform them of God's decrees and laws.' Moses' father-in-law replied, 'What you are doing is not good. You and these people who come to you will only wear yourselves out. The work is too heavy for you; you cannot handle it alone. Listen now to me and I will give you some advice, and may God be with you. You must be the people's representative before God and bring their disputes to him. Teach them the decrees and laws, and show them the way to live and the duties they are to perform. But select capable men from all the people—men who fear God, trustworthy men who hate dishonest gain—and appoint them as officials over thousands, hundreds, fifties and tens. Have them serve as judges for the people at all times, but have them bring every difficult case to you; the simple cases they can decide themselves. That will make your load lighter, because they will share it with you. If you do this and God so commands, you will be able to stand the strain, and all these people will go home satisfied.' Moses listened to his father-in-law and did everything he said" (*Exodus 18:13-24*).

REFLECT: The Lord doesn't want us to merely survive as we serve Him and those He loves; He wants us to *thrive*. Ask Jesus to show you how you are doing personally, emotionally, and in your relationships with Him. Pause until you can hear His voice; then record His words to you:

Now ask others who are close to you how they think you are doing personally, emotionally, spiritually, and in your relationship with your family and friends. Listen carefully to what they say; then record your spouse and/or closest friend's words to you:

To help you see if you are currently *surviving* or *thriving* in ministry, respond honestly to the following statements with T (true), F (false), or S (sometimes).

_____ I have good co-laborers who support me in my work as an Activist.

_____ I don't lack energy or enthusiasm for what I do.

_____ My relationship with God is strong and vibrant.

_____ Depression is not an issue for me.

_____ I have a good counselor I feel comfortable talking with at anytime whose name is_____ .

_____ I keep the Sabbath weekly by_____.

_____ I have several friends I can be "off" with, folks I spend time just hanging out with at least three times a month (*not* doing work or ministry) named_____.

_____ My financial resources are strong.

_____ I go away by myself to rest and pray at least one day each month by going to_____.

_____ I take time for hobbies and have enjoyed several activities this month, such as_____.

_____ In addition to my weekly Sabbath, I take at least three days off work each month to_____.

_____ I have at least ten people right now who've volunteered or been asked to pray for my family and me regularly named_____
_____
_____.

_____ My feelings of love for the marginalized and oppressed are strong.

_____ I have good mentors—like Moses' father-in-law—who speak into my life on a consistent basis named_____.

RESPOND: What did you learn about your current health and well being through answering these questions and talking to those closest to you?

Ask the Lord to show you what you need to do now to build a strategy for thriving in life and ministry. List the steps here or in your journal:

If it would be helpful, what mentor or group of Activists/non-Activists can you approach this week to add balance to your life?

RECORD: Describe the action you took this week?

How did you see or feel Jesus' presence with you?

What follow-up still needs to be done?

Share your experience with a friend you can trust, asking her to check in with you next month about how your 'thrival strategy' is coming.

Write a prayer now committing your steps to the Lord (see Psalm 37:5).

Week 3 ~ **The Activist** ~

INTEGRATION: Review the last few weeks. What has God taught you?

How will your life be different because of what you've learned?

If there are ways you need to take action in the future, write them here or in your journal.

Now receive God's total grace and reflect upon His unalterable love for you—no matter how you think you did as you worked on these spiritual exercises.

2

The Ascetic
Loving God through Solitude and Simplicity

Intermediate Spiritual Practices for the Ascetic

Week 1 ~ **The Ascetic** ~

READ: The Bible is indeed God's love letter to His people—the infallible, *God-breathed* record of His acts throughout history (see 2 Timothy 3:16). Yet God calls us to go beyond knowing and studying scripture; He calls us to know and study *Him* (see John 17:3 and Luke 15:8). And as we do, His Spirit promises to transform us and make us more and more like Him (see 2 Corinthians 3:18).

Sadly, one of my friends told me that even though he graduated from Bible school and seminary at the top of his class, it took a spiritual crisis in his life to free him to "pursue a relationship with a Person—Jesus—instead of just knowing a book." Our fathers and mothers of the faith understood this vital merger of Spirit and Word through their practice of *lectio divina*, or "spiritual reading." A second-century monk named Guigo II first articulated the four steps of *lectio divina* when he wrote this letter to a friend:

> One day when I was busy working with my hands, I began to think about our spiritual work, and all at once four stages in spiritual exercise came into my mind: reading, meditation, prayer and contemplation. These make a ladder for monks by which they are lifted up from earth to heaven. It has a few rungs, yet its length is immense and wonderful, for its lower end rests upon the earth, but its top pierces the clouds and touches heavenly secrets.[6]

In lectio or spiritual reading, the Bible becomes a conduit of God's Spirit, a means for God to speak to us and bring His truth to our hearts and minds in that moment. *Lectio* includes the following steps:
- *Reading*—paying careful attention to God in the Scriptures.
- *Meditation*—applying the mind to seek God and His and hidden truth.

---

[6] Guigo II, The Ladder of Monks: A Letter on the Contemplative Life and Twelve Meditations, translated By Edmund College and James Walsh (Kalamazoo, Mich.: Cistercian Publications, 1979), 67–68.

- *Prayer*—turning the heart to God to drive away evil and obtain what is good.
- *Contemplation*—lifting the mind to God so that it "tastes the joys of everlasting sweetness."[7] Thus we read (*lectio*) under the eye of God (*meditatio*) until our heart leaps (*oratio/prayer*) and bursts into a flame of delight (*contemplatio*).

REFLECT: Describe your method and motivation for reading the Bible:

As important as it is to know God's Word, how free do you feel to have a relationship with a Person—Jesus—instead of just reading His Word?

In the following areas, rank how your current method of reading Scripture helps you know the Lord more deeply *(1 is low; 5 is high):*

_____ The Bible helps me commune with God and pay close attention to Him.

_____ Scripture is one way the Lord reveals Himself and His mysteries to me.

_____ God's Word helps me practice the Lord's presence all day long.

_____ I am transformed by scripture, and am becoming more like Jesus through reading and meditating on it.

_____ I am strengthened to resist temptation and live fully yielded to Christ by reading His Word.

_____ The Bible stirs me to worship and adore the Lord, fanning my spiritual passion for Jesus

If you were to tell someone how scripture is currently blessing you and "lifting you from earth to heaven", what would you say?

---

[7] Guigo II, *The Ladder of Monks: A Letter on the Contemplative Life* and *Twelve Meditations*, 68

RESPOND: Now try utilizing *lectio divina* as you read the story in Luke 15:11-32.

Lectio: In your Bible, read the story first with your imagination, inviting the Spirit to use your God-given, God-surrendered mind's eye to transport you to the time and place of the story. Your creative mind may recreate the story in a contemporary context, or you may see the setting as you imagine it was in Jesus' day. Now read the passage again, only this time read aloud slowly and thoughtfully, allowing pictures to be formed in your mind as you hear the words. (Take 15 minutes or longer for this.)

Meditatio: Reflect now upon what you've just read. Ponder the ideas and insights communicated in the passage. *Feel* your way into the text, personalizing your reading and considering what it means to you. Where do you see yourself in the story? As you read the parable in the present moment, do you identify with the wayward younger brother, or the self-satisfied older son? Perhaps you felt more kinship with the father, or maybe you saw yourself as an onlooker, someone invited (or not invited) to the party. Reflect upon what this reveals to you about yourself and your interaction with God. If Jesus were with you right now telling you the story as He did to the disciples, what more might He want to say to you? (Allow up to 20 minutes.)

Oratio: Speak to God about this experience. Having read the text aloud and having brought it to life by pondering its meaning, now begin a highly personal dialogue with God. A profound bonding and a deeper, transformative healing occur when you use the Scripture to talk to God about your life. Tell Him what you heard, saw, experienced, and received from the passage. Share your feelings and thoughts with Him, your insights and concerns, your questions about things that are unclear. Thank Him for any instructions you received from Him, and tell Him what you intend to do now. Ask for what you want because of His message to you. (Allow 10-30 minutes.)[8]

Contemplatio: Now sit quietly with the Lord. This is the last step: a time to simply receive from Him what He wants to give you—His grace, forgiveness, love, and quiet presence. This is not a time to talk, but to just be with God, ready to listen

---

[8] For those having trouble getting started on this, your response may sound something like: God, I wish I had a father like the one in this story. Such mercy. I feel like the Prodigal, running away from responsibility and often living life for myself. Even though I am Your child and I know You love me, I have trouble believing that You could want me close to You, that You are waiting and watching for me to come, that You run to meet me and want to celebrate my life as I approach You. But Lord, interestingly, I also see myself as the older brother. I, too, feel resentful that in life I carry so much of the burden while others just seem to get by doing so little. Dear God, please take away the bitterness that is poisoning me and replace it with Your love and grace. Help me when I'm feeling jealous of others or when I'm miffed that my efforts go unnoticed. Make me like You, Father God, generous of heart and willing to give sacrificially.

and receive. Be attentive to God's Spirit in and with you. Focus on Him and just sit quietly in His abiding presence. (Allow ten to thirty minutes.)

As you repeat this exercise throughout the week, you may want to go through this same passage using the *lectio* format, or choose another passage such as Luke 15:4-7, or Luke 15:8-10.

RECORD: How would you describe your experience doing *lectio divina* this week?

How has your relationship with Jesus changed as you've read Scripture with Him this way?

Share your experience with a friend you can trust, asking him to check in with you next month to see how *lectio divina* is enriching your time with God through His Word.

Write a prayer, committing your steps to the Lord (see Psalm 37:5).

READ: Just as Socrates said, "Know thyself," Saint Augustine said, "Lord, let me know myself, and let me know Thee!" Many of our early church fathers and mothers were proponents of this "double knowing"—believing that all Christian growth came from knowing the Lord and knowing ourselves. John Calvin focuses on this in his Institutes, highlighting that the deeper one's walk with God, the deeper one's reflective life and study of self must be, including one's faults, limitations, moral weaknesses, and inadequacies. This degree of self-awareness creates a channel for God's grace to flood the humble, repentant heart.

It's also believed that this extent of self-knowing cannot be done in isolation. The Benedictine, Joan Chittister, writes, "Alone, I am what I am, but in community I have the chance to become everything that I can be."[9] In community, serious believers have long sought spiritual feedback from companions and guides who travel with them on the inward and outward journey, helping them know the Lord and themselves more correctly.

One way to find spiritual companionship is through acquiring a spiritual director, someone on the path who has walked ahead of you, someone who is able to listen with wisdom and grace as God develops new habits in your heart. Trained in the art of spiritual discernment and listening, Margaret Guenther likens a spiritual director to a "midwife of the soul," a guardian who is present during times of spiritual vulnerability, offering support and feedback at every stage as the new life God is being formed and birthed in us.[10]

During times when I've had spiritual directors, I've often come with complicated questions—things that were hanging me up—and together we've come to the Lord, then waited on Him for clarity. The spiritual directors who've walked with me have greatly encouraged me in the 'spiritual birthing' process.

REFLECT: If you do not already have a spiritual director, would you like to find a person who is able to put himself aside so that his total attention is focused on what God is doing in your life?

---

[9] Joan Chittister, *Wisdom Distilled from the Daily: Living the Rule of Saint Benedict Today* (San Francisco: Harper San Francisco, 1990), 49.
[10] Margaret Guenther, *Holy Listening* (Boston: Cowley Publications, 1992), 82–93.

If so, where is there a church or monastery in your area that you might find a person trained in this way?

RESPOND: If you are eager to find a spiritual director, begin the process by asking the Lord to lead you to a person He knows will be helpful to you. Then read Margaret Guenther's book, *Holy Listening,* and decide if there is someone in your life currently who could become (or help you find) a spiritual director.

RECORD: How did you actively seek finding a spiritual director this week?

How did you see Jesus leading you in this process?

What are your next steps in finding someone to help you know God and yourself more accurately?

Share your experience with a friend you can trust, asking her to check in with you next month about how spiritual direction is going, and what you are learning from walking with a spiritual director.

Write a prayer now committing your steps to the Lord (see Psalm 37:5).

INTEGRATION: Review the last two weeks. What has God been teaching you?

How will you utilize what you've learned in the coming months?

If there are ways you need to take action in the future, write them here or in your journal.

Advanced Spiritual Practices for the Ascetic

Week 1 ~ **The Ascetic** ~

READ: Though Ascetics need a regular sense of apartness in order to experience the Lord's presence, they also have a high value for community because they realize that it is only in fellowship with others—even those who may be challenging—that God's Spirit transformed His people into the image of Christ. Thus, Ascetics wisely utilize a commitment to community to offset any tendency to isolate or be excessively alone. As Larry Crabb said, "As surely as birds were made to fly and fish to swim, we were made for community, for the kind of community the Trinity enjoys, for spiritual community. And to the degree we experience it, we change, we grow, we heal."[11]

God Himself is communal; He is Triune—three in one. And He created humankind, who is the pinnacle of His handiwork, to be inescapably communal as well, reflecting in union the image of the Triune God. We depend on others to be born, to live, to multiply, to survive, be buried, and to be remembered. We all must live in community in order to grow, however sparse or challenging that community may be.[12]

There are many factors in our culture today, however, that work against our dedication to community, causing us to believe and act as if:

> "…faith and salvation were essentially private, acultural and ahistorical… an individual concern, something that gives color to our private lives but is not publicly accountable. What I think or feel about God is between my conscience and me. 'Spirituality' is an amorphous, ever mutable engagement between two isolated selves—the human individual and 'God,' both apart from the world, change, time, place and community." [13]

Though this is what our culture suggests, spiritual formation has never been a private affair; it is a community project, with each of us being an instrument of God's Spirit to one another.[14] Personal freedom reaches its greatest meaning when viewed within an assortment of accountable spiritual relationships. Here, Father, Son, and Spirit teach us that convergence is essential because it's only in the presence (and through the pressure) of others that we become who we were truly meant to be—Christ's body *together*.[15]

REFLECT: If growing in Christ is a community project, how are you seeking an assortment of accountable relationships in your life?

Who are these people (go ahead and name names)?

[11] Larry Crabb, *The Safest Place on Earth: Where People Connect and Are Forever Changed* (Thomas Nelson, 1999), 124.

[12] Rodney Clapp, *A Peculiar People: The Church as Culture in a Post-Christian Society* (IVP, 1996), 194.

[13] Clapp, 34, 36.

[14] Stanley J. Grenz, *Theology for the Community of God* (Eerdmans, 2000), 496–497.

[15] Norvene Vest, *Friend of the Soul: A Benedictine Spirituality of Work* (Cowley Publications, 1997), 115.

Together, how are you attending to one another's hearts, minds, and spiritual growth?

How might you do a better, more intentional job of this with one another?

RESPOND: In Trinitarian fashion, find two people this week with whom you would like to form a six-month accountability relationship (a "triad") for the purpose of pursuing an ongoing renovation of the heart. Don't select people quickly; pray and see who God brings to mind. Then when you come together, be prepared to share your responses to the questions you are pondering in life. Some triads don't need prewritten questions, but if they would help you, here are a few questions that may help you get started:

- What truth affected you most from either a spoken message or your study in God's Word since we last met?
- How have you sensed God leading you, and what action is He inviting you to take—in partnership with Him?
- How is your intimate life—spiritual and soul intimacy with your spouse, your children, or your closest friends—becoming more like that of the Trinity?
- How are you pursuing greater spiritual and soul intimacy with God?
- How are you contributing to God's mission by being His light and salt in your world?
- What are you reinvesting in others that the Lord has invested in you?
- How are you showing excellence on the job?
- In what ways can we support each other in those areas where God's Spirit is inviting us to change?
- What challenges are you facing that you would like us to pray with you about?

RECORD: How did you take action this week to form a community of accountable relationships?

How did you experience the Lord's presence as you searched for and hopefully found those with whom to build community?

What follow-up do you still need to do?

Share your experience with a friend you can trust, asking her to check in with you next month about how your triad is progressing, and what you are learning from one another.

Write a prayer now committing your steps to the Lord (see Psalm 37:5).

Week 2 ~ **The Ascetic** ~

READ: Ascetics have a high esteem for the discipline of submission, which is the willingness to yield to others because the value for the good of all comes before their own. This is not a weak, mindless deference, but a strong, caring response that requires great inner fortitude; it is wisdom that is peace loving, gentle, and willing to yield (see James 3:17). This type of submission demonstrates love that is not self-seeking love, but, with humility of mind, regards others as more important than self (see Philippians 2:3). It is indeed true Christlikeness!

Today, godly submission tends to be counter-cultural, yet God says it is an essential aspect of becoming mature in Christ. Even the Son of God had to learn obedience through submission (see Heb. 5:7-8 and Luke 22:42).

It involves not only a surrender to God; it includes how we listen to those in our own community. This requires that we learn to give up our way and accept the common voice of wisdom and truth—even when it's difficult—in order to gain greater freedom through obedience. The Benedictines held a strong conviction that the way we submit to one another revealed how we submitted to God.[16] Esther deWaal reflects:

> "Subjecting myself to another 'in all obedience for the love of God' means giving up my power, my arrogance, and instead submitting myself to seek the will of God through others. If I want to grow, openness and interaction with others is imperative, since then I can grow with the help of someone else's gifts. I admit my limitations and my weakness, and I let someone else hold me up so I can go on. This of course prevents any false self-image and cuts down my pride in my own sufficiency." [17]

This growth is the gift submission brings. Richard Foster says that when we gain "the ability to lay down the terrible burden of always needing to get our own way. . . . submission can free us sufficiently to distinguish between genuine issues and stubborn self-will. Then, in submission, we are at last free to value other people." [18]

Yes, Christ made us free, "not freedom to do wrong, but freedom to love and serve each other" (*Galatians 5:1, 13, TLB*). In this state we are at last free *from* ourselves and free *for* God, which is the greatest freedom of all!

REFLECT: As you look at your own pattern of decision-making within community, how willing are you to yield in loving wisdom to others—your spouse, your friends, even your children? Place an "N" on the continuum representing where you are NOW.

autonomous and self-governing   *harmonious and cooperative*

⟵——————————————————————————⟶

---

[16] Brent Peery, "Benedictine Spirituality Contextualized for Evangelical Christians" (DMin. dissertation, Azusa Pacific University, 2002), 83.

[17] Esther DeWaal, *Seeking God: The Way of Saint Benedict* (Collegeville, Minn.: The Liturgical Press, 1984), 47.

[18] Richard Foster, *Celebration of Discipline* (San Francisco: Harper, 1978), 111–113.

Then place an "L" on the continuum to represent where you'd LIKE to be as your heart bows more consistently to Jesus.[19]

RESPOND: In Proverbs we are told that feedback is a very important tool for becoming wise, even when it comes in the form of correction (see Proverbs 6:23, 10:17, 12:1, 13:18, 15:5, 10, 12, 32, 29:15). Show this exercise to those in your community, including your family, your accountability partners, and others you trust. Invite them to place their initials on your continuum based on how they experience you submitting within community. Thank them for having the courage to be honest, even if you disagree with their perspective. Discuss with them the "L" you gave yourself, and invite their feedback, both now and in the future—giving them permission to speak into your life anytime they think it would help you move forward. Listen to their comments in silence; try to take seriously what they are saying—even when you are prone to disagree, become defensive, or disregard their input.[20]

Then dialogue with God about your ability to submit to others, not just those in authority, but to others around you. Listen carefully to what the Lord has to say to you about this, especially regarding the feedback you received from your friends and family. Ask Him to help you move toward greater Christlikeness in the area of submission—with Him, those in your household, and your community.

RECORD: Describe the feedback you received from your friends and family about how they view your ability to submit.

---

[19] In present day society (which some have called the "ME generation"), autonomy and self-governance are highly valued. And there is nothing intrinsically wrong with these, until our independence and self-rule conflicts with God's Word and ways. He is the One who commands that we walk in humble union with Himself and others, living in harmony, sympathy, love, and compassion (see Romans 12:16; 1 Peter 3:8).
[20] When the prophet Nathan told David that God would establish His throne and Kingdom through him, God also said, "I will be a Father to him and he will be a son to Me; when he commits iniquity, I will correct him with the *rod of men*" (2 Samuel 7:14, NASB). The Lord often uses people—those who know the Lord and those who don't—to be His *rod of correction* in our lives, and He corrects us because of His mercy and love.

What did you learn about yourself from asking for feedback?

How did the Lord say about your ability to walk in submission to Him and others?

Where and how would you like to grow in the area of submission?

Talk with God now about your desire to be more like Jesus.
Share your intentions with a friend you can trust, asking him to check in with you next month about your progress in appropriate submission to others.

Write a prayer, committing your steps to the Lord (see Psalm 37:5).

Week 3 ~ **The Ascetic** ~

INTEGRATION: Review the last two weeks. What has God taught you?

How will the lessons you learned become a permanent part of your life?

If there are additional steps for you to take, write them here or in your journal.

Now receive God's grace and reflect upon His unalterable love for you—no matter how you feel you did on these spiritual exercises these past few weeks.

3

The Caregiver
Loving God through Serving Others

Intermediate Spiritual Practices for the Caregiver

Week 1 ~ **The Caregiver** *~*

READ: For the Caregiver, shouldering the burdens of others is a form of worship. These know the truth of the gospel when Jesus taught, "Whatever you did for one of the least of these brothers of mine, you did for Me" *(Matthew 25:40)*. Mother Teresa, a consummate caregiver, taught us to look behind the eyes of the poor, the sick, and the needy to the eyes of God, and love Him by caring for those He loved. She once said, "At the end of life we will not be judged by how many diplomas we have received, how much money we have made, how many great things we have done. We will be judged by, 'I was hungry, and you gave me something to eat; I was naked and you clothed me; I was homeless, and you took me in."[21]

REFLECT: Who are the "least of these" in your life—those who require care but have little or nothing to give in return?

What attitude might God be inviting you to have in serving these people (seeing His face, His eyes, His heart in and through them)? How can you show love in a new way, as if you were caring for Jesus as you care for them?

---

[21] https://www.goodreads.com/author/quotes/838305.Mother_Teresa

RESPOND: If specific people came to mind, list the names of people Jesus is leading you to care for—those whom you may need to see differently.

Ask God now for the grace to care for these people as you would care for Him—to serve Him as you serve them. List ways you plan to show each person God's heart.

RECORD: What new attitudes and actions did you see in yourself this week?

How did this transformation in your heart make you feel?

What do you still need God to do in your life so that you can love the "least of these" as Jesus loves them… and as *He loves you?*

Share your progress with a friend you can trust, asking her to check in with you next month about your new attitudes and actions toward "the least of these."

Write a prayer, committing your steps to the Lord (see Psalm 37:5).

Week 2 ~ **The Caregiver** ~

READ: In his book, *Conspiracy of Kindness*, Steve Sjogren suggests that it would be good for Christians to combine service with evangelism by doing random acts of kindness: deeds of service done without any specific reason or context. He proposes that Christ-followers actually look for ways to bless those who do not follow Jesus, such as raking leaves for a neighbor, shoveling snow on a stranger's sidewalk, or giving out cookies on a university campus.[22] These random acts of kindness become an indirect way of pointing their recipients to the kindness of God

REFLECT: When you consider God's kindness to you through others, list some specific acts of care that stand out in your mind?

RESPOND: This week, write a thank you note to as many people as you can who've shown God's kindness to you. List them here or in your journal:

---

[22] Steve Sjogren, *Conspiracy of Kindness* (Ann Arbor, Mich.: Servant, 1993).

Then pray for, notice, and respond to at least five random (unplanned) opportunities to show kindness to others—preferably things others will not know you did. As you do these random deeds, note the attitude of your heart.

Ask the Lord to teach you to better reflect His kindness to others, making your deeds an act of worship to the Father (who surprises us often with undeserved kindness).

RECORD: Describe your attempts at doing random acts of kindness this week:

What did you learn about yourself in the process?

Where do you still need to grow?

Share your progress with a friend you can trust, asking him to check in with you to see how your random acts of kindness and your heart condition are becoming more like Jesus'.

Write a prayer, committing your steps to the Lord (see Psalm 37:5).

INTEGRATION: Review the last two weeks. What has God taught you?

How will you make what you learned a regular part of your life?

If there are ways you need to take action in the future, write them here or in your journal.

Advanced Spiritual Practices for the Caregiver

Week 1 ~ **The Caregiver** ~

READ: The Bible instructs us on how to be good Caregivers:

> "Be devoted to one another in brotherly love. Honor one another above yourselves. Never be lacking in zeal, but keep your spiritual fervor, serving the Lord. Be joyful in hope, patient in affliction, faithful in prayer. Share with God's people who are in need. Practice hospitality. Bless those who persecute you; bless and do not curse. Rejoice with those who rejoice; mourn with those who mourn. Live in harmony with one another. Do not be proud, but be willing to associate with people of low position. Do not be conceited. Do not repay anyone evil for evil. Be careful to do what is right in the eyes of everybody. If it is possible, as far as it depends on you, live at peace with everyone" (*Romans 12:10-18*).

REFLECT: On a scale of 1 to 5, consider how you give care to others in the following areas (*1 is low; 5 is high*):

_____ Being devoted to others in brotherly love
_____ Honoring others above yourself
_____ Zealously serving the Lord as you serve others
_____ Being joyful, hopeful, and patient with others
_____ Praying faithfully for others
_____ Sharing with God's people who have financial and practical needs
_____ Practicing hospitality
_____ Blessing those who persecute you
_____ Rejoicing with those who rejoice and mourning with those who mourn
_____ Living in harmony with others
_____ Being teachable, humble, and open-minded
_____ Associating with the those of a low social status
_____ Not being smug, vain, or self-satisfied

RESPOND: Show your numbers to someone you trust and ask if they think you are seeing yourself accurately. If this person cannot confirm your numbers, ask her to share what she sees. You will have a chance to practice being teachable, humble, and open-minded when listening to her feedback.

Select one area from the list in which you especially need to grow. Write it here, and how you plan to partner with the Lord to see transformation take place:

Then write Romans 12:10-18 on three-by-five cards and carry them with you this week. As you meditate on the passage, ask God to give you an opportunity to practice caring with this attitude.

Plan to take action this week in one of the areas above where you scored 3 or below. For example, if the area is hospitality, invite someone (you would not normally spend time with) to your house for lunch, dinner, or dessert. Start small if you need to—in other words, you may want to invite someone from church or from your neighborhood whom you don't know well, as opposed to a homeless person. On the other hand, if God prompts you to take a bigger step and care for someone living on the streets, be sensitive and follow His leading. What is your plan?

RECORD: How did you take action this week in the area of caring for others?

If you felt stretched, what did you see God do in your heart?

How did God bless others through you?

Share your progress with a friend you can trust, asking her to check in with you next month about this situation and the action you took.

Write a prayer, committing your steps to the Lord (see Psalm 37:5).

Week 2 ~ **The Caregiver** ~

READ: On the day before His death, Jesus—the most profound Caregiver of all time—gave us an amazing picture of what it looks like to serve others. Even in the midst of His own impending crucifixion, Jesus was caring for his own:

> "Jesus, knowing that the Father had given all things into His hands, and that He had come forth from God and was going back to God, got up from supper, and laid aside His garments; and taking a towel, He girded Himself. Then He poured water into the basin, and began to wash the disciples' feet and to wipe them with the towel with which He was girded. . . . He said to them, "Do you know what I have done to you? You call Me Teacher and Lord; and you are right, for so I am. If I then, the Lord and the Teacher, washed your feet, you also ought to wash one

another's feet. For I gave you an example that you also should do as I did to you. Truly, truly, I say to you, a slave is not greater than his master, nor is one who is sent greater than the one who sent him. If you know these things, you are blessed if you do them" *(John 13:3-5, 12-17, NASB).*

REFLECT: Why do you think Jesus washed the disciples' feet that night?

Jesus invites us to join Him in this humble act of service. But since most of the people we have contact with wear shoes (and drive cars), how is Jesus' example of removing the travelers' dirt applicable in your life today?

Jesus not only washed John the Beloved's feet, He also washed Judas's feet. He didn't just demonstrate care for those who loved Him and with whom He shared affection; He also cared for those who had their own agenda and ultimately betrayed Him. Ask God how you might apply this principle of unconditional love and humble service in your life by caring for those you feel close to *and* those who don't have your best interests in mind.

Who will you serve in your home, church, or neighborhood?

RESPOND: In solidarity with Jesus, take time this week to wash the feet of those who look to you for leadership. If you are a pastor or business leader, find a way to "wash the feet of your staff," figuratively if necessary, but literally if possible. If you are a father or mother, wash the feet of those in your family. If no one looks to you for leadership, select people you might serve by washing their feet like Jesus did. Who comes to mind"

If you are able to make this exercise a literal foot washing, what will you say to introduce and explain why you are doing this activity in a way that will bless those whose feet you wash?

If you work in an environment with people who do not yet know the Lord and would not understand this gesture, ask God to give you an alternate way to serve them, still demonstration a care-giving spirit. Try to select an act of kindness that will cost you more *time* than *money* and will increase your humility and love for others so that they sense your care for them.

RECORD: How did you emulate Jesus' example this week by "washing the feet" of those who look to you, either literally or figuratively?

How did that feel?

What did you learn about yourself in this process?

What did you learn about the Lord?

What did you learn about the people whose feet you washed?

Share this experience with a friend you can trust, asking him to check in with you next month about how you are continuing to "wash the feet of others."

Write a prayer, committing your steps to the Lord (see Psalm 37:5).

Week 3 ~ **The Caregiver** ~

INTEGRATION: Review the last two weeks. What has God taught you?

How will you continue applying what you learned?

Are there ways you need to take action in the future? If so, write them in your journal.

Now receive God's total grace and reflect upon His unalterable love for you—no matter how you did completing these spiritual exercises the last few weeks.

4

The Contemplative
Loving God through Adoration

Intermediate Spiritual Practices for the Contemplative

Week 1 ~ **The Contemplative** ~

READ: The first inclination of a person with a Contemplative Spiritual Temperament is to draw near to God. Often extravagant lovers of Jesus, Contemplatives feel comfortable using the language of lovers to talk openly about their intimacy with Him. They enjoy extended time in God's presence gazing into His face, so is it any wonder that an ancient form of intimate prayer is known as "contemplative prayer"?

A Christian practice given by our desert mothers and fathers, contemplative prayer is a gift to the church that is not widely talked about in evangelical circles today. In this type of prayer we do not primarily relate to God as the One sitting on His throne in heaven, but as the One dwelling on the throne of our hearts. Here the focus is on seeing and knowing God up-close-and-personally, which the Bible invites us to do:

> "One thing I ask of the LORD, this is what I seek: that I may dwell in the house of the LORD all the days of my life, to gaze upon the beauty of the LORD and to seek Him in His temple" *(Psalm 27:4).*

> "And we, who with unveiled faces all reflect the Lord's glory, are being transformed into His likeness with ever-increasing glory, which comes from the Lord, who is the Spirit" *(2 Corinthians 3:18).*

> "Keep your eyes on Jesus, who both began and finished this race we're in. Study how He did it. Because He never lost sight of where He was headed—that exhilarating finish in and with God—He could put up with anything along the way: cross, shame, whatever. And now He's *there*, in the place of honor, right alongside God" *(Hebrews 12:2, The Message).*

> "Be still, and know that I am God" *(Psalm 46:10).*

Richard Foster, a renowned author on the subject of prayer, describes contemplative prayer in three progressive stages: recollection, the prayer of quiet, and spiritual ecstasy.[23] Though there are similarities and overlapping characteristics between the phases, here is a description of each:

•*Recollection* happens when we come intentionally to God, letting go of all that distracts us from our devotion to Jesus. As we gain an inner knowing of God's love, we turn away from everything external to focus on the Lord's presence in that moment. Resting in the quiet, we invite the Holy Spirit to make Himself real, perhaps by envisioning Jesus sitting across from us in a chair (since He truly *is* present, but sometimes we need to visualize that reality); then we use our God-given, God-sanctified imagination to surrender our whole selves to the Lord for His pleasure, purpose, and glory. This is a taste of what Brother Lawrence called "practicing the presence of God." [24]

•*The prayer of quiet* is the second phase in contemplative prayer. In recollection we learned to put away all obstacles of the heart, all distractions of the mind, and all vacillations of the will. Divine graces of love and adoration washed over us like ocean waves, and at the center of our being we were hushed. It's then that we can experience a "listening stillness" because something deep inside is awakened and brought to attention; it's as if our spirit is alert and on tiptoe, anticipating God's divine whisper. We linger with Jesus as if to absorb His presence into every fiber of our begin, and as we go on our way, we carry His presence with us; just as smoke is absorbed into clothing and carries its smell, so the aroma of God's seeps into our being, and makes us carriers of His fragrance throughout the day.[25]

•The third phase of contemplative prayer is *spiritual ecstasy.* This comes when we calmly wait in passive repose. In that place of detachment from all that's around us, we are granted illumination: a spirit of revelation from God. It's here that He satisfies us with the light of His love in such a way that we are overwhelmed and captured by Jesus' presence and peace. We may even feel "spiritually inebriated," and as if we're being lifted to another plain.

Ultimately, the goal of contemplative prayer is not an experience, but Christ Himself. As we learn to be still, commune with Him, and rest knowing He is God, we realize that we were created for fellowship—even union—with the Lord, and nothing else will satisfy.

---

[23] This section is adapted from Richard Foster's book, *Prayer: Finding the Heart's True Home* (HarperOne, 2002).

[24] Brother Lawrence, *The Practice of the Presence of God* (Whitaker House: New Abridged edition, 1982).

[25] Thanks to James W. Goll, author of, *The Lost Art of Intercession,* and *Kneeling on the Promises,* for his summary of contemplative prayer. For more information, visit encountersnetwork.com.

REFLECT: As you consider the three stages of contemplative prayer, how is the Lord stirring you to want more in your prayer life?

Which aspect of contemplative prayer might be helpful for you in developing a more intimate relationship with God (underline or highlight those aspects most desired)?

> •*Recollection*: letting go of all competing distractions, gaining an inner knowing of God's love for you, turning away from all else to focus on God's presence while resting in quietness, asking the Holy Spirit to make Himself real to you, or envisioning the Lord sitting across from you in a chair as you "practice His presence".

> •*The prayer of quiet*: learning to put away all obstacles of the heart, all distractions of the mind, and all vacillations of the will until His divine grace of love and adoration washes over you like an ocean wave and you are hushed, experiencing a "listening stillness" and anticipation of God's divine whisper, carrying His fragrance everywhere you go.

> •*Spiritual ecstasy*: being calm in passive repose, detached from all that's around you, experiencing illumination and revelation from God as you are overwhelmed and captured with Jesus' presence and peace, feeling "spiritually inebriated" as if lifted to another plain.

Describe now how you would like to know the Lord more intimately:

RESPOND: Begin by taking the next step. Reread the description of contemplative prayer with its three phases. Spend at least 15 minutes seeking God in the prayer of Recollection, the Prayer of Quiet, or Spiritual Ecstasy. Ask the

Lord to give you the grace to press in.[26] Don't hold anything back from Him, and confess every temptation to desire anything other than Him. When distractions come, release them to God without giving them your attention, just as if you were sitting on your front porch and all of your worries, fears, thoughts, and tasks were merely cats strolling by. Do not call the cats over to you or allow them to sit on your lap. Just let them walk by until they are out of sight. Keep your focus on the Lord, noting how He is present to you.

End your time by talking with Jesus about your desire to know Him so that His fragrance permeates your being and is detectable everywhere you go.

RECORD: How was your hunger for God stirred this week as you practiced contemplative prayer?

What would you like to ask the Lord to do in your heart and mind to increase your hunger for Him?

Share this experience with a friend you can trust, asking her to check in with you next month to see how you are doing in your face-to-face encounters with Jesus.

---

[26] *Pressing in,* as I call it, happens when we move closer to God — in spite of the discomfort or uneasiness we feel. Just as blind Bartimaeus *pressed in* to Jesus (though the crowd told him to keep quiet, see Mark 10:46-52), and just as the woman with the hemorrhage of blood *pressed in* to touch Jesus' robe (though social and religious customs dictated otherwise, see Mark 5:25-34), so we *press in* with this same determination, moving past all obstacles in or around us. It's as if we're on the tenth floor of a burning building and the elevator is going down for the last time. When the door opens on our floor and we see that the elevator is already full, our desperation for life motivates us to *press in* because there's no other way out of the building! Our desire to live trumps social customs, the opinions of others, or even our own awkwardness about stepping into an elevator full of people! When we want breakthrough that badly, we will *press in* to God for it! And thankfully, He rewards those who diligently seek Him (see Hebrews 11:6).

Write a prayer, committing your steps to the Lord (see Psalm 37:5).

Week 2 ~ **The Contemplative ~**

READ: Thomas Merton said that contemplation is the desire for union with God as our inmost self pursues "a quest for Him Who is above all, and in all, and Who Alone is Alone."[27] Union with God is the goal of our lives; that's what Jesus prayed for when He asked that we would "be one, just as You and I are one—as You are in me, Father, and I am in You" (*John 17:21, NLT*). Oneness with God is our ultimate destination—in this life and the next.

Teresa of Avila described 'holy union' as an interior castle where God is at the center. As we approach Him, we come to live in greater communion with Him, and our lives are given over to our loving Lord, including regular times of deep, adoring silence. Motives are purified as we become aware of God's holiness and our sinfulness; worship and work become intertwined because both are expressions of God's life flowing through us. This is the life Jesus prayed we would experience with the Godhead—Father, Son, and Spirit.

REFLECT: Ponder Merton's words that the One "Who is above all, and in all, and Who Alone is Alone" is indeed the magnificent, transcendent One who is profoundly other in His holiness and power and knowledge. He alone has absolute authority, command, and dominion. Then consider that this God, the Creator and Sustainer of life, has come to earth as Immanuel—God with us— that He draws us close, speaks to us, prays for us, reunites us to the Father, and will never leave or forsake us (see Matthew 11:28; John 10:27; Hebrews 7:25; Romans 5:11; Hebrews 13:5).

Take a moment to consider the decision of the transcendent God to become immanent, to take on flesh and come near so He could be present *to us and in us,*

---

[27] Thomas Merton, *The Inner Experience: Notes on Contemplation* (San Francisco: Harper, 1959), 30.

to be constantly attentive, accessible, active, and daily engaged—moment-by-moment—with us…forever.

How does it feel to belong to this One who is nearer to us than breath?

RESPOND: This week, write John 17:20-23 on a three-by-five card. Carry it with you so that at every opportunity—when you are stopping at an intersection in your car, waiting in line, sitting between appointments—you can meditate on the truth that God invites you to become *one with Him*, just as Jesus is one with the Father.

Since Jesus would not have prayed for something He did not expect to happen, what do you think oneness with God needs to look like in your life?

How might you cooperate more consistently with Him in His desire for oneness *with you?*

Talk with God now about the truth that Jesus wants this oneness, prayed for it, and made it possible for us to experience increasing union with Him.

RECORD: Describe what happened in your heart this week as you meditated on the truth that God is transcendent (above everything) yet immanent (dwelling right here with us):

What did you learn as you focused on the One who invites—no, *expects* and *provides for*—your union with Him?

How did His invitation to be one with Him effect you?

Share your experience with a friend you can trust, asking him to check in with you next month about how oneness with God is slowly transforming you.

Write a prayer, committing your steps to the Lord (see Psalm 37:5).

Week 3 ~ The Contemplative ~

INTEGRATION: Review the last two weeks. What has God been teaching you?

How will you integrate what you have learned about God's desire to be one with you into your life?

If there are ways you need to take action in the future, write them here or in your journal.

Advanced Spiritual Practices for the Contemplative

Week 1 ~ **The Contemplative** ~

READ: In Scripture, the idea of having a full, productive life while regularly beholding the Lord's face was the way those who loved God anticipated living. The Bible says this about the face of God:

- "Seek the Lord and His strength; seek *His face* continually" *(Psalm 105:4, NASB)*.
- The Lord spoke to Moses *face-to-face*, as a man speaks with his friend (see Exodus 33:11).
- "The Lord bless you and keep you; the Lord make *His face* shine upon you and be gracious to you; the Lord turn *His face* toward you and give you peace" *(Numbers 6:24-26)*.
- "When Gideon realized that it was the angel of the Lord, he exclaimed, "Ah, Sovereign Lord! I have seen the angel of the Lord *face to face*!" *(Judges 6:22)*.
- "Do not hide *Your face* from your servant; answer me quickly, for I am in trouble" *(Psalm 69:17)*.
- "Because I am righteous, I will see You. When I awake, I will see You *face to face* and be satisfied" *(Psalm 17:15, NLT)*.
- "When You said, 'Seek *My face*,' my heart said to You, '*Your face*, O Lord, I shall seek'" *(Psalm 27:8, NASB)*.

The Lord takes pleasure in face-to-face encounters with us; He enjoys looking into *our* faces and scrutinizing *our* ways (see Psalm 139). He also invites us to look into *His* face and scrutinize *His* ways. Gazing at Him, we become lost in His love and forget ourselves—our blunders and the blunders of others. The only thing we see is God: His tender eyes; His gentle, affectionate, and affirming smile; His strength, grace, and longing for us. We are transformed by beholding Him with an unveiled face (see 2 Corinthians 3:18). As the psalmist said, "It was not by their sword that they won the land, nor did their arm bring them victory; it was Your right hand, Your arm, and the light of *Your face*, for You loved them" (Psalm 44:3).

REFLECT: Jesus said, "An hour is coming, and now is, when the true worshipers will worship the Father in spirit and truth; for such people the Father seeks to be His worshipers. God is spirit, and those who worship Him must worship in spirit and truth" *(John 4:23-24, NASB)*. As you consider that God is spirit, what do you think He intends when He invites us to *seek His face?*

Why do you think it's important?

What is special to you about *a face?*

RESPOND: Think of a person whose face you enjoy seeing, a person whose face usually makes you happy. Who comes to mind?

What is it about their face that you enjoy most?

Here or in your journal, draw this person's face (or write the words that come to mind when you look at her)—physical characteristics or inner attributes you can see:

Now spend a few moments quietly seeking the Lord's face. Ask Him to reveal His characteristics or inner attributes, those aspects of Himself you might not otherwise see. Write what He reveals to you as you gaze at *His face*:

RECORD: In what ways did God reveal *His face* to you this week?

Tell the Lord about your desire to see and know Him *face-to-face:*

Now listen for His response. Write it here:

Share this experience with a friend you can trust, asking her to check in with you next month about how you are doing in seeking and encountering the Lord face-to-face.

Write a prayer, committing your steps to the Lord (see Psalm 37:5).

READ: For centuries, people of faith have looked to Ignatius of Loyola as a spiritual father. In his writing, Ignatius described two fundamental spiritual conditions of the heart: one he called *Consolation* and the other he referred to as *Desolation*. These are not feelings or emotions, but like other conditions, they will have accompanying feelings and emotions that often indicate what is going on at a deeper level.[28]

Ignatius defined *Consolation* as the presence of enlivening feelings for God demonstrated when we find ourselves shedding "tears of love for our Lord, whether out of sorrow for our sins or for the Passion of Christ, or because of other things directly connected with His service and praise. Consolation is every increase of hope, faith and charity, and all interior joy that calls us to heavenly things, giving us peace in our Creator and Lord."[29] Ignatius taught that Consolation was never ours to achieve or possess, but only God's to give.

In contrast, *Desolation* brings feelings of death; it is contrary to Consolation in that it is expressed in a "prevailing love for things low and earthly, the unquiet of different temptations, a lack of confidence in God, when we love not God, when we find ourselves all lazy, tepid, and sad, as if separated from our Creator and Lord."[30] Desolation reflects the "troubled heart" Jesus described to His disciples (see John 14:27), and is not given to us by God.

Sometimes Christians believe that if they are doing everything correctly, all will be well and they will continually sense God's presence, grow in ever-increasing intimacy, and be filled with joy. Conversely, they believe that when Desolation comes, it must be because they are doing something wrong. But the truth is that Desolation is a condition brought on by many factors, including—but not limited to—our sinful nature and the temptations of Satan. While Desolation may well follow the willful blocking of God's Spirit through carnal behavior or attitudes, according to Ignatius, Desolation doesn't always follow rebellion. Yes, "the rebellious dwell in a parched land" *(Psalm 68:6, NASB)*, but Desolation also comes because we live in a fallen world. Thus, we experience the results of our fallenness and the fallenness of others whose lives affect us—namely those who have lived before us and prepared the way. We see this when, in His darkest hour, the sinless Christ experienced Desolation, saying, "My God, my God, why have You forsaken me?" (Mark 15:34). Desolation comes to all of us this side of heaven.

---

[28] Many thanks to Dr. Tom Ashbrook and Imago Christi for their work on the article, "Discernment: Discovering God's Will – Personally and Together", June 2012

[29] James Wakefield, *Sacred Listening* (Grand Rapids, Mich.: Baker Books, 2006), 43–44.

[30] Wakefield, 44.

Though Desolation is certainly not desirable, Ignatius taught that God uses it to expose conditions of the heart that need attention, challenging us to live by faith without the blessing of God's "felt presence." When Consolation is absent, or when dark nights of the senses or soul prevail (as described by the 16th-century mystic, Saint John of the Cross),[31] even then we must live and obey God by faith in His goodness. Thus, when there is no light to comfort us, we learn persistence and patience, and our love for God is given an opportunity to deepen and be purified. It is only then that we realize that peaceful trust in God's character is all that's required for our happiness; nothing more is ultimately needed to sustain us.

REFLECT: Developing an ever-deepening relationship with God calls for an understanding of our overall journey with Him. Think back to times in your life when you were experiencing Consolation (feelings of hope, faith, joy, and enthusiastic love for God). List some of those times here or in your journal:

Desolation (times of temptation, lack of confidence in God, spiritual laziness, half-heartedness, indifference, apathy, and sadness) occurs in life, too. List some of the times you experienced Desolation:

RESPOND: Use the timeline below to represent your relationship with God—from birth on the left to present day on the right. Divide the line into five or ten year increments. Draw some symbols on the time line to reflect your spiritual story (for example, you could draw a cross for the moment you gave your life to

---

[31] St. John of the Cross, *Dark Night of the Soul* (Dover Publications, 2003).

Jesus). Be creative, using symbols or pictures that have meaning to you to depict your significant times with God, both positive and negative.

Birth  Present

Now using this as a baseline, graph your times of Consolation above the line: times when you experienced the nearness of God. The greater the intimacy and Consolation experienced, the higher you place your symbol or picture above the line.

Then graph your times of Desolation using symbols or pictures drawn below the line: seasons when you were unaware of God's presence and love, even though you may have been walking with Jesus. Make this graph the story of your spiritual journey thus far.[32]

Ignatius taught that Desolation can be a useful tool in helping us become indifferent—even detached—from all that hinders our relationship with God. He maintained that indifference is necessary because:

> We were created to praise, reverence and serve God, our Lord, and by
> this means to experience salvation; all things on earth are created for us
> and are beneficial only as they help us praise, reverence and serve God.
> We are to use them only as much as they help us in our praise, reverence
> and service, and we ought to rid ourselves of anything that hinders that
> praise, reverence and service. For this, it is necessary that we become
> indifferent to all created things so that, on our part, we want not health

---

[32] Thanks to Church Resource Ministries, my friend and colleague Dave Jackson, and the Imago Christi Team for developing this exercise.

rather than sickness, riches rather than poverty, honor rather than dishonor, long rather than short life, desiring and choosing only that which helps us praise, reverence and serve God. This detachment will come only if we have a stronger attachment. Therefore our one dominating desire and fundamental choice must be to constantly abide in the living presence and wisdom of Christ, our Savior.[33]

Looking back over your life, draw a dotted circle around seasons or events when you were experiencing Desolation, yet now look back and see that God was taking your roots deeper into Him, helping you detach from everything except Jesus:

> "Blessed are those who trust in the Lord and have made the Lord their hope and confidence. They are like trees planted along a riverbank, with roots that reach deep into the water. Such trees are not bothered by the heat or worried by long months of drought. Their leaves stay green, and they never stop producing fruit" *(Jeremiah 17:7-8, NLT).*

What were you learning from/about the Lord during those dry or difficult times?

Talk with Jesus now about how He was present during these seasons—ways He may even now be inviting you into a new place of expanded grace. Dialogue with the Lord about this, then listen for His response. Write His words here or in your journal:

---

[33] Ignatius of Loyola, "Principle and Foundation", adapted from a handout in Catherine Gregg's class on Ignatian Spirituality, July 2002, Azusa Pacific University. Ignatius' "Principle and Foundation" also states that God loves us and wants to share His life with us. Our love response takes shape in the way we praise, honor, and serve God, making Him the center of our lives. All the things in this world are created because of God's love, and they become His gifts to us so that we can know God more easily and return His love more readily. As a result, we show reverence for all the gifts of creation. "But if we abuse any or make it the center of our lives, we break our relationship with God and hinder our growth as loving persons. We must learn to hold ourselves in balance so that our only desire and one choice should be this: I want and I choose what better leads to God's deepening life in me."

RECORD: What did God show you this week as you contemplated your life, and how Consolation and Desolation have effected you?

What did you learn about the Lord from your timeline?

What did you learn about yourself?

Share your experience with a friend you can trust, asking him to check in with you next month about how consolation and desolation are affecting your life with God.

Write a prayer, committing your steps to the Lord (see Psalm 37:5).

Week 3 ~ **The Contemplative** ~

INTEGRATION: Review the last two weeks. What has God shown you?

How will you take what you have learned and make it a part of your life from now on?

If there are ways you need to take action in the future, write them here or in your journal.

Now receive God's total grace and reflect upon His unalterable love for you—no matter how you feel you did on these spiritual exercises the last few weeks.

5
The Enthusiast
Loving God through Mystery and Celebration

Intermediate Spiritual Practices for the Enthusiast

Week 1 ~ **The Enthusiast** ~

READ: People with Enthusiast Spiritual Temperaments tend to love God with great gusto. Known as the 'cheerleaders' of the faith, they often feel closest to God when worshipping Him in the congregation, which for them is 'party time'. Praise and worship is a valued part of their life with the Lord, and something they do... 'enthusiastically'!

This kind of enthusiastic worship is found throughout the Bible, where the word *worship* appears more than a hundred times, and the word *praise* appears in over two hundred passages. Praise and worship are core components in our relationship with God because everyone was created to worship—and indeed we *will* worship someone or something, whether it's the true God or not.

The word *worship* in the New Testament—*proskuneo*—means "to move toward" (*pros*) and "kiss" (*kuneo*).[34] Inherent in worship is the notion of bringing our whole selves to the Lord Jesus, moving toward Him in abandonment and holy affection. Though Biblical worship often included a specific time and place set apart for God's people to offer themselves wholly while attending to Him, in Hebrew culture, worship never stopped; it was a life-style, an ongoing commitment to love "the Lord with all your heart and with all your soul and with all your strength and with all your mind" (Luke 10:27). Worship was not merely a weekly event because all of life was an act of devotion to God. As the Apostle Paul instructed:

> "Let the word of Christ dwell in you richly as you teach and admonish one another with all wisdom, and as you sing psalms, hymns and spiritual songs with gratitude in your hearts to God. And whatever you do, whether in word or deed, do it all in the name of the Lord Jesus, giving thanks to God the Father through Him" (*Colossians 3:16-17*).

Thus, everything we do to serve and bring pleasure to Jesus becomes worship!

---

[34] W. E. Vine, *An Expository Dictionary of New Testament Words*, Volume IV (Revell, 1966), 235.

REFLECT: Describe how, when, and in what situations you turn your heart and mind toward the Lord for an extended time, meditating on Him, expressing your love to Him, especially when no one is leading you to do this.

How comfortable are you conveying deep feelings of affection to the Lord, allowing love and passion for Him to arise in your heart?

In what ways to you desire to see praise and worship become your life-style?

RESPOND: Though praise and worship go beyond music, they also involve singing psalms, hymns and spiritual songs with gratitude in our hearts to God (see Colossians 3:16). This week practice expressing holy affection and love to Jesus by reading aloud the words of this song to Him. As you do, offer Him your love in whatever way you want to express it:

> No other Lover could ever discover the hope and the longing
> I keep in my heart.
> Only You, Jesus, could fill every longing,
> Only You, Jesus, could meet every need.
> You are kindness and compassion, full of mercy, full of grace,
> And I love when You so tenderly hold me in Your embrace.
> Always faithful, ever able, bringing healing to my soul,
> You're my laughter, You're my treasure,
> You're my song of songs, strong and true,
> I belong to only You.
> You are Daystar; You are Dawning, Light of lights, Joy of joys,
> You are Kingdom, You are Power, You are Glory, You are Lord.[35]

---

[35] Andrea Hunter and Marty Goetz, "Only You, Jesus," *Healing Presence*, Life Unto Life Music, 1996, Singin' in the Rain Music.

This week borrow or purchase a CD, or download an MP3 album, with a collection of songs containing intimate dialogue with the Lord. If you aren't sure which CDs fit this description, ask a friend, or someone at your church or local Christian bookstore for a recommendation. Then find a comfortable place where you won't be interrupted to listen to the CD, inviting the Lord to open your heart to Him so you can both give affection *to* Him and receive affection *from* Him. This is sometimes referred to as "soaking" in the Lord's presence. Practice soaking often this week.[36]

RECORD: How would you describe your times of worshipping God this week?

What will you ask the Lord to help you do in the future so that your love and affection for Him will flow more freely?

Share your experience with a friend you can trust, asking her to check in with you next month about your heart of worship toward God.

Write a prayer, committing your steps to the Lord (see Psalm 37:5).

Week 2 ~ **The Enthusiast** ~

READ: Enthusiasts are comfortable with the mystical aspects of God and Christian spirituality. They feel free to explore the supernatural, and don't avoid those expressions of the faith that, although reasonable, are sometimes hard to explain. Author and teacher Eugene Peterson writes:

---

[36] Interestingly, when my dishes are dirty, I often let them soak in warm, soapy water in the sink. Then when I remove the food later, it comes off more quickly. This is one of the benefits of listening to Christian music and "soaking" in the Lord's presence. Besides simply relaxing and enjoying God and His great love for us, soaking tends to soften our hearts, allowing all that needs to go to be washed away more quickly by the Water of His Word and Spirit.

There is a huge world that we have not yet seen, an incredible creation that we cannot account for, a complex reality that is not defined or controlled by our experience of it. There is more—far more. Our experience, while authentic enough, is not encompassing. There is far more that we don't know than what we do know.[37]

Prayer, too, contains an aspect of mystery. How can someone in California petition God to protect a friend in Kenya, and have that provision come within moments of the request... even though a literal ocean lies between them? Like electricity, we may not be able to understand exactly how it works, but we can still flip the switch and use it to light our homes! So it is with prayer: "a gift, a mystery made up of moments of experience." [38]

REFLECT: When it comes to those aspects of God that are invisible and beyond our understanding, some people ignore those things, while others compose theological structures around them, or reduce them to a Christian cliché to explain them away, such as: "God must have His reasons," or "God works in mysterious ways." How do you handle the unexplainable, those aspects of God's spiritual realm that you don't fully comprehend?

When you doubt what you can't see or understand—especially when it comes to the obscure, ungraspable workings of God—how do you process or resolve that tension?

Psalm 103:7 tells us that while God made His *acts* known to the children of Israel (i.e., what He did), He showed Moses His *ways* (i.e., how and why He did things). God took Moses backstage, so to speak, and revealed to him His own heart and mind.

Today, the Lord is still revealing Himself—His character, even His Kingdom secrets—to those who sincerely want to know Him.[39] Ephesians 1:17 tells us that

---

[37] Eugene Peterson, *Subversive Spirituality* (Vancouver, B.C.: Regent College, 1994), 21.
[38] Moore and Maguire, *The Experience of Prayer* (London: Darton, Longman & Todd, 1969), 103–104.
[39]Dan. 2:28: "There is a God in heaven who *reveals mysteries.*" Matt. 13:11 (NASB): "Jesus said to them, 'To you it has been granted to *know the mysteries* of the kingdom of heaven.'" 1 Cor. 4:1 (NASB): "Let a man regard us in this manner, as servants of Christ and stewards of the *mysteries of God.*"

God will give us "the Spirit of wisdom and revelation, so that [we] may know Him better." What mysteries or unanswered questions would you like to better understand, aspects of the Lord's ways that might be troubling you, or things you are uneasy about?

Is there someone in your life you can talk with about your questions—a mature spiritual friend who knows the Lord deeply and might help you make sense of some of your questions and doubts? If so, who comes to mind?

List a few of the questions you might want to ask this person:

RESPOND: Call your spiritual friend this week and ask her if you can get together soon. If she lives out of town, set up a phone conversation or Skype call to talk about your questions. Share some of your questions in advance so she can think and pray about them beforehand.

RECORD: How was your time with your spiritual friend this week?

What did you learn?

If you would like to meet with this person again (perhaps on a regular basis), ask God to prepare the way for that to happen.

Share your progress into the mysteries of God with someone you can trust, asking him to check in with you next month about how you are processing the unexplainable.

Write a prayer, committing your steps to the Lord (see Psalm 37:5).

Week 3 ~ **The Enthusiast** ~

INTEGRATION: Review the last two weeks. What has God taught you?

How will you integrate what you have learned into your life?

If there are ways you need to take action in the future, write them here or in your journal.

Advanced Spiritual Practices for the Enthusiast

Week 1 ~ **The Enthusiast** ~

READ: As we've already stated, worship is every act of devotion to the Lord that is done with our whole person—body, soul, and spirit. And because the Lord has granted us His favor, we can actually minister to Him when we worship Him by attending to God's greatness and celebrating His worth. That's why we sometimes have to respond physically when we worship: we feel compelled to raise our hands, or we sense a shout coming on, or we need to bow low, or offer to dance as an intentional act of praise to our great and awesome God! As the Psalmist said:

> "Shout for joy to the Lord, all the earth. Worship the Lord with gladness; come before Him with joyful songs. Know that the Lord is God. It is He who made us, and we are His; we are His people, the sheep of His pasture. Enter His gates with thanksgiving and His courts with praise; give thanks to Him and praise His name. For the Lord is good and His love endures forever; His faithfulness continues through all generations" *(Psalm 100:1-5)*.

In Scripture, we see that some worshipers stood to their feet when they encountered the presence of God (see Deuteronomy 29:10); some lifted their hands (see 1 Timothy 2:8); some clapped (see Psalm 47:1); some shouted (see Ezra 3:11); some fell prostrate (see Revelation 19:10). Many people danced as an act of worship: Miriam, Moses' sister and the women of Israel danced with tambourines (see Ex. 15:20); King David celebrated the ark entering Jerusalem with leaping and dancing before the Lord (see 2 Samuel 6:16, 1 Chronicles 15:29).

In fact, the Bible records that when God moves powerfully in the lives of His people, dancing is anticipated:

> "The young women will dance for joy, and the men—old and young— will join in the celebration. I will turn their mourning into joy. I will comfort them and exchange their sorrow for rejoicing" *(Jeremiah 31:13, NLT)*.

Yes, dancing is a part of how we use our bodies to worship God; it's always been how God's people demonstrated love for their Lord, and it's how we continue to express jubilation in His presence (see Psalm 149:3, Psalm 150:4).

Interestingly, tradition teaches that *God Himself* dances! In the seventh century, Syrian theologian John of Damascus described the relationship of the Trinity as a *perichoresis*, a "circle dance." *Choros* is an ancient Greek round dance performed at banquets and festive occasions. John envisioned the Godhead as a holy community, a circle in which existed a sense of joy, freedom, song, intimacy, celebration, and harmony—and we have been invited in!

REFLECT: How comfortable are you using your whole body to worship God?

What moves you to stand, raise your hands, clap, bow, shout, lie prostrate, dance, or use your body in other ways to worship God?

The psalmist said, "Praise His name with dancing and make music to Him with tambourine and harp. . . . Praise him with tambourine and dancing" *(Psalm 149:3; 150:4)*. Have you ever danced before the Lord, allowing your body to express your deep love for God?

If yes, describe that experience?

If no, how would it be to dance before the Lord in a private place where you felt you were truly offering praise and worship to Jesus?

RESPOND: Practice worshipping God this week with your whole body. Play one of your favorite praise albums and listen closely to the words. Sing along only as it helps you express your love for God. More importantly, allow the words to soak in and saturate your heart. If they indicate standing or bowing, allow your body to assume that posture before God.

As different thoughts and emotions come to mind, raise your hands high or stretch them wide to signify your abandonment and utter devotion to Jesus. Let your body move in whatever way feels like a sincere expression of express worship and praise. With only Jesus watching, how pleased He is by your full surrender, especially when you offer Him a "sacrifice of praise" (see Hebrews 13:15). If you feel awkward or silly, try to "press in" past that feeling.[40] *Pressing in* is how we move beyond obstacles that are in or around us holding us back, past social customs that keep us boxed in, beyond the opinions of others, or even further than our own awkward feelings in order to seek Jesus, who promises that if we seek Him, we will definitely find Him (see Luke 11:9). Practice this exercise often this week.

---

[40]As was stated earlier, *pressing in,* as I call it, happens when we move closer to God — in spite of the discomfort or uneasiness we feel. Just as blind Bartimaeus *pressed in* to Jesus (though the crowd told him to keep quiet, see Mark 10:46-52), and just as the woman with the hemorrhage of blood *pressed in* to touch Jesus' robe (though social and religious customs dictated otherwise, see Mark 5:25-34), so we *press in* with this same determination, moving past all obstacles in or around us. It's as if we're on the tenth floor of a burning building and the elevator is going down for the last time. When the door opens on our floor and we see that the elevator is already full, our desperation for life motivates us to *press in* because there's no other way out of the building! Our desire to live trumps social customs, the opinions of others, or even our own awkwardness about stepping into an elevator full of people! When we want breakthrough that badly, we will *press in* to God for it! And thankfully, He rewards those who diligently seek Him (see Hebrews 11:6).

RECORD: How did you experience worshipping God—body, soul, and spirit?

How did you *press in* past your feelings—as if meeting God were a matter of life or death?

In what ways did you experience Jesus being present with you all week long?

Share your experience with a friend you can trust, asking him to check in with you next month about how you are worshiping God with your whole being—body, soul, and spirit. .

Write a prayer now committing your steps to the Lord (see Psalm 37:5).

Week 2 ~ The Enthusiast ~

READ: No matter how much an Enthusiast enjoys worshipping God and celebrating His goodness, everyone who resides on planet earth finds his 'spiritual mountaintop experience' dwindling at one point or another. That is because we live in a fallen world with a system that opposes our Father God (and an enemy who likes to take his fury out on our Father's kids—us!). And though Paul tells us in Romans 8:37 that we are more than conquerors through Him who loved us, the process of growing to be like our Big Brother, Jesus, is not an easy one…

since we were intended to be "fully mature adults, fully developed within and without, fully alive like Christ" *(Eph 4:13, The Message)*. This process of development applies to all God's people. *Even Jesus,* who was anointed with the oil of joy above all others (see Psalm 45:7), had to grow and develop, which not only included increasing in wisdom, stature, and favor with God and men (see Luke 2:40), but also meant being tested in the wilderness (see Matthew 4:1), and learning to trust and obey His Abba through what He suffered (see Hebrews 5:8). Here's how the Bible describes our life-long growth process:

> "All around us we observe a pregnant creation. The difficult times of pain throughout the world are simply birth pangs. But it's not only around us; it's within us. The Spirit of God is arousing us within. We're also feeling the birth pangs. These sterile and barren bodies of ours are yearning for full deliverance. That is why waiting does not diminish us, any more than waiting diminishes a pregnant mother. We are enlarged in the waiting. We, of course, don't see what is enlarging us. But the longer we wait, the larger we become, and the more joyful our expectancy" *(Romans 8:22-25, The Message).*

Because the long-term goal of our faith-development is Christlikeness, the Bible describes this heart-and-mind renovation in three phases:[41]

•We begin *as little children*, growing in our awareness of who we are as sons and daughters of God, realizing the benefits of having been adopted into the Royal Family—now fully accepted in the Beloved—with an eternal inheritance that includes eternal forgiveness of all our sins (see 1 John 2:12).

•Then we grow into *young men and women* in the faith, gaining strength and maturity, internalizing God's Word, and understanding spiritual warfare more clearly as we walk more and more consistently in the power of God's Spirit (see 1 John 2:14).

•As spiritual *mothers and fathers* in the faith, we continue to experience a deep, abiding love relationship with the Godhead, bearing fruit steadily because our lives are defined by the fixed presence of Jesus, our coming Bridegroom and King (see 1 John 2:13). The challenging Kingdom work God gives us to do— the good works God prepared for us in advance (see Ephesians 2:10)—now flow from our lives with less effort and more grace.

---

[41] This exercise contains general spiritual formation principles that apply to all the spiritual temperaments. They are, however, especially helpful to Enthusiasts—who highly value experiencing and celebrating God's presence—in order to assist them in embracing the challenges they'll face in the life-long process of growing into the fullness of Christ, and the discipline that maturity requires.

REFLECT: Think back to some of the most challenging growth times in your life, seasons where you had to choose joy amidst the difficulties of becoming mature. Describe one of those times here or in your journal, including how you felt and reacted:

What did you learn about God and about yourself during that time?

When you consider the phase of development you are currently in, would you consider yourself to be a child in the faith? A young man or woman? Or a Mother or Father in the faith? Why?

RESPOND: Here are some important questions for you to ask yourself at each phase:

Young children:
   • How is your realization of being God's child increasing, and how are you seeing that truth become a part of your interactions every day?

   • When you experience struggles within and without, how real is your awareness of God's grace—experiencing the Lord's forgiveness even when you know you don't deserve it?
   • How are you developing a life-style of discipleship, including a growing desire to please and honor God, know His Word, and lovingly interact with others in God's family?

   • How is your daily life becoming more characterized by God's love, joy, peace, and grace (doing good *from* God's love rather than *for* God's love), and less about Christian rules (minding the "shoulds" and "should not's," avoiding guilt, etc.)?

Young Men and Women
> • As you more fully comprehend kingdom realities, how are you allowing God's Spirit to fill and guide you?
>
> • How are you dealing with more subtle temptations (pride, jealously, envy, etc.) as God discloses your motivations and invites you to internalize His grace (vs. just manage your sin or improve your behavior)?
>
> • How are you balancing opportunities to serve God with time spent enjoying Him?
>
> • How are you becoming more aware of spiritual warfare, knowing when and how to put on the full armor of God (see Ephesians 6:11-18)?

Fathers and Mothers in the Faith:
> • How are you attending to your deep longing for intimacy with the triune God, i.e., making time and space to respond to God's desire for greater oneness?
>
> • How have you been "seeing" and experiencing God in all of life, transitioning from *doing* to *being*, from serving to loving, responding to God's presence in every moment of your day?
>
> • How has your time in prayer changed, becoming more intuitive and responsive?
>
> • How are you growing through finding or becoming a spiritual director?

RECORD: What are you learning about yourself in this season of spiritual life?

What needs to happen next to grow into greater and maturity?

Share what you've been learning with a friend you can trust, asking her to check back next month to see how your pursuit of God and Christlikeness is coming.

Write a prayer, committing your steps to the Lord (see Psalm 37:5).

Week 3 ~ **The Enthusiast** ~

INTEGRATION: Review the last two weeks. What has God been teaching you and doing in your life?

How will you continue to move closer to the Lord in the future?

If there are things you need to do next, write them here or in your journal.

Now receive God's total grace and reflect upon His unalterable love for you—no matter how you feel you did on these spiritual exercises the last few weeks.

6

The Intellectual
Loving God through the Mind

Intermediate Spiritual Practices for the Intellectual

Week 1 ~ The Intellectual ~

READ: When Jesus said we need to love the Lord our God with all our minds (see Mark 12:30), He was speaking the love language of those with an Intellectual Spiritual Temperament. For them, loving God comes through the intellect where their faith needs to be understood as much as experienced. Intellectuals enjoy learning new things about God, reading the latest Christian books, or taking classes and seminars on spiritual topics, because for them, "right thinking" is essential.

Interestingly, the Bible makes an intriguing statement: "Using a dull ax requires great strength, so sharpen the blade. That's the value of wisdom; it helps you succeed" (*Ecclesiastes 10:10, NLT*). In *The Message*, here's how this verse appears: "Remember: the duller the ax the harder the work; Use your head: the more brains, the less muscle."

REFLECT: Ponder what you think this verse means.

In terms of the Intellectual Spiritual Temperament, what is your "ax," and how might it need sharpening?

My pastor-friend, George Haraksin, defines wisdom as an experiential understanding of how to live happily, deeply, and in harmony with God, oneself, others, and the cosmos. Describe your value for wisdom, including what makes it especially important in your life?

Thinking back over your life, when and in what ways has wisdom given you success?

How has ignoring wisdom caused you trouble?

RESPOND: Ask one of your pastor-friends to have lunch with you this week—preferably one who challenges you to think more deeply about spiritual things. At lunch, ask this pastor how she stays sharp mentally   how she "sharpens her ax." Inquire about books this pastor has been reading or would recommend, and about any seminars she's planning to attend. If these books or seminars interest you, purchase one of the books or plan to attend a seminar. Then, after you've read the book or attended the seminar, buy lunch for your pastor friend again. This time, discuss what you've learned and how your thinking and spiritual life have been challenged and "sharpened".

RECORD: Describe how your time with your pastor friend encouraged and motivated you spiritually?

How do you plan to keep sharpening your ax?

How might you more intentionally pursue wisdom in the future—and the success it brings?

Share your pursuit with a friend you can trust, asking him to check in with you next month about your longing for wisdom and the action you are taking.

Write a prayer, committing your steps to the Lord (see Psalm 37:5).

Week 2 ~ **The Intellectual** ~

READ: During Old Testament times, Ezra was a man who vigorously studied the Word of God. He devoted himself to examining and observing the Law, then teaching the nation of Israel its judgments and precepts (see Ezra 7:10). When a Hebrew studied or taught the Torah, that meant he was dedicated to knowing and understanding Jehovah's deeper message—to carefully and faithfully examining and probing the ancient manuscripts for God's fuller intention and meaning.

We are encouraged to vigorously study the Word of God as well. And as we are diligent to present ourselves to God as those who don't need to be ashamed because we know how to accurately handle the word of truth (see 2 Timothy 1:15, NASB), we, too, can come to know and understand God's fuller intention and meaning.

Thomas Brooks, a seventeenth-century preacher, said,

> "It is not the mere touching of the flower by the bee that gathers honey, but her abiding for a time on the flower that draws out the sweet. It is not he that reads most, but he that meditates most, that will prove to be the choicest, sweetest, wisest, and strongest Christian." [42]

In other words, to really understand God's word, study and meditation are required.

REFLECT: What biblical stories, words, or themes have you wanted to study more carefully (for example, God's glory, the fear of the Lord, forgiveness, caring for the poor, Jesus' healing ministry, God's sovereignty, etc.)?

---

[42] Thomas Brooks, *The Complete Works of Thomas Brooks*, Puritan Press.

What specifically do you want to know about this topic, and why is this important to you?

When you are interested in a Bible topic, what has worked best for you in learning more about that (for example, searching the Bible? Talking with friends? Looking in commentaries? Reading books? Listening to podcasts? Memorizing scripture? Praying and asking God for greater insight, etc.)?

RESPOND: Begin this week to study a specific word or topic that is of interest to you. You will need several tools: Bibles in more than one version (for example, NIV, NASB, *The Message*, The New Living Translation, etc.), an exhaustive Bible concordance, a Bible dictionary and commentary. As you open God's Word and other books, pray that the Lord will give you greater understanding of who He is and His ways. These steps may be helpful:

1. Select your word or topic and look up that word (and all relevant and corresponding words) in your Bible dictionary.

2. Look up the word or topic in your exhaustive concordance, finding each time the word is used in Scripture. Read and take notes on as many passages as possible.

3. Compare the word or topic in different versions of the Bible. For example, compare the following versions of John 1:14 and see how each gives a slightly different flavor to the Incarnation:

    "And the Word became flesh, and dwelt among us, and we saw His glory, glory as of the only begotten from the Father, full of grace and truth" *(NASB)*.

    "So the Word became human and made His home among us. He was full of unfailing love and faithfulness. And we have seen His glory, the glory of the Father's one and only Son" *(NLT)*.

"The Word became flesh and blood, and moved into the neighborhood. We saw the glory with our own eyes, the one-of-a-kind glory, like Father, like Son, generous inside and out, true from start to finish" *(The Message)*.

4. From your study thus far, discern what you understand the word or verses to mean. Come to your own conclusions before you look up your word or topic in a Bible commentary and study what scholars have said about it.

5. Find other books that have been written on this topic, and talk with trusted friends about what you are learning.

6. Pray and meditate on what you are learning, asking the Lord to show you more of Himself as you study.

RECORD: What did God show you about Himself as you studied this week?

What did you learn about yourself?

How will your life be different from the understanding you've gained about the Lord through the topic you studied?

Share your study with a friend you can trust, asking him to check in with you next month about this topic and the effect it is having on your life.

Write a prayer, committing your steps to the Lord (see Psalm 37:5).

Week 3 ~ The Intellectual ~

INTEGRATION: Review the last two weeks. What has God taught you?

How will you integrate what you have learned into your life?

If there are ways you need to take action in the future, write them here or in your journal.

Advanced Spiritual Practices For the Intellectual

Week 2 ~ The Intellectual ~

READ: The book of Proverbs tells us that just as iron sharpens iron (two substances of equal sturdiness honing and polishing the other), so friends can sharpen, challenge, and polish one another (see Proverbs 27:17). This verse brings to mind two equally matched warriors sparring with their swords, building up one another's strength, skill, and capacity during practice as they challenge each other before the war begins.

A person with an Intellectual Spiritual Temperament is especially prone to need friends who can provoke her thinking—people of equal capacity who can stimulate her thinking as well as speak the truth in love. This sparring may occur during a hearty spiritual discussion or through personal words of exhortation and challenge. Ephesians says, "Speaking the truth in love, we will in all things grow up into him who is the Head, that is, Christ" (*Ephesians 4:15*).

REFLECT: Who in your life challenges you to think more deeply or differently, someone who exhorts you, speaks the truth in love to you, and causes you to step out of your comfort zone? Name the people here:

Now write down the names of people who may have real truth to speak into your life, those to whom you enjoy talking and listening, but who currently are not challenging or 'sparring with' you?

How can you intentionally cultivate more consistent contact with one or more people from your list(s)?

RESPOND: This week, initiate a conversation with a friend with whom you are equally matched in some capacity, a person who is not afraid to challenge your thinking or speak the truth to you in love. When you're talking to this person, ask God to open your heart and mind to receive the truth from your friend, and if difficult things are said, ask the Lord to give you the grace to take to heart this word of wisdom: "Whoever loves discipline loves knowledge, but he who hates correction is stupid" (*Proverbs 12:1*).

RECORD: With whom did you initiate a mentally (and perhaps emotionally) challenging conversation this week, and how did you "spar"?

How was your thinking challenged in beneficial ways?

Did the encounter become an intellectual debate, or did you experience it as a dialogue that carried with it a personal challenge from the Lord?

What was most difficult for you about the conversation?

How do you anticipate growing and changing from this experience?

How will you internationalize these meetings so that sparring becomes a regular part of your life?

Ask God now to give you the grace to receive the truth from others so that you can grow from their feedback, both those who are like iron sharpening you, and from those who have something valuable to say even though their presentation may not be as sharp as yours.

Share your growing edges with a friend you can trust, asking her to check in with you next month to see how you are both sparing and receiving the truth from those around you.

Write a prayer, committing your steps to the Lord (see Psalm 37:5).

READ: There's an old song by Jim Croche called, **"I'll Have To Say I Love You In A Song,"** because—as the song reveals—every time the writer tried to express his love, the words just came out wrong. That's the way it can be in our lives, too. When we try to express our love for God, there are times when no words seem adequate, especially for those who are better at evaluation and analyzation. Our minds remain so busy, so full of thoughts, that they have trouble stopping long enough for us to access our hearts, allowing us to speak and listen to words of love from the heart.

Of course, stopping and accessing our hearts is precisely the kind of vulnerability (and loss of control!) we need if we want to learn to *be with God*— enjoying His presence, allowing our minds to relax and even receive from Him—and eventually move past being *wordy and active* with Him, to being *wordless and receptive* to Him.

God instructs us to come to Him with a heart that is able to, "*Cease striving* and know that I am God" *(Psalm 46:10, NASB, emphasis added)*. The Hebrew words for "cease striving" literally mean to "be still, relax, let go and fall limp." God is not only asking us to give Him our lives; He is asking us to give Him our *minds*, to come to the point where we can relax our intellects because we are confident that *He is God!* Thus, we can stop believing it's our responsibility to figure everything out, and begin to let ourselves rest in the arms of a very big God who is exquisitely brilliant. As we are told in Deuteronomy 33:27, "The eternal God is your refuge, and underneath are the everlasting arms."

REFLECT: How good are you at turning off the flow of words in your mind—even during prayer—so you can truly *be still, relax your mind, let go, and fall limp* with God, receiving whatever He has for you?

What would it take for you to cease striving so that your mind could *be still, relax, let go and fall limp*?

If the idea of letting go makes you uneasy, consider Jesus' invitation, and ponder what it might look like to cease striving. He said:

> "Are you tired? Worn out? Burned out on religion? Come to Me. Get away with Me and you'll recover your life. I'll show you how to take a

real rest. Walk with Me and work with Me—watch how I do it. Learn the unforced rhythms of grace. I won't lay anything heavy or ill fitting on you. Keep company with Me and you'll learn to live freely and lightly" (*Matthew 11:28-30, The Message*).

What might it look like for you to come get away with Jesus and let Him show you how to take a real rest; to walk and work with Him, watching how He does it as you learn the unforced rhythms of grace?

RESPOND: Spend some time now with the Lord. If you have a hammock or a place to recline, go there to rest, picturing yourself being held by the Lord as He supports all your weight. You are not too heavy for Him. As you begin, open your heart in this quiet place to receive whatever God has for you. Ask for His agenda and not your own. Now read the words of Psalm 46:1-11 (NASB):

> God is our refuge and strength, a very present help in trouble.
> Therefore we will not fear, though the earth should change
> And though the mountains slip into the heart of the sea;
> Though its waters roar and foam,
> though the mountains quake at its swelling pride.
> There is a river whose streams make glad the city of God,
> The holy dwelling places of the Most High.
> God is in the midst of her, she will not be moved;
> God will help her when morning dawns.
> The nations made an uproar, the kingdoms tottered;
> He raised His voice, the earth melted.
> The Lord of hosts is with us; The God of Jacob is our stronghold.
> Come, behold the works of the Lord,
> who has wrought desolations in the earth.
> He makes wars to cease to the end of the earth;
> He breaks the bow and cuts the spear in two;
> He burns the chariots with fire.
> Cease striving and know that I am God; I will be exalted among the nations,
> I will be exalted in the earth. The Lord of hosts is with us;
> the God of Jacob is our stronghold.

Now take time to be still and do nothing; simply be quiet and rest in the presence of God. Invite His Spirit to rest in and on you. If a word or phrase caught your attention as you read the passage, slowly and gently allow the Lord to bring an image to your mind's eye if He should choose. Let His Spirit lead your time together. Listen for what He may want to say to you, and if something comforting comes to your heart or mind, stay there with Him as long as possible. If your mind begins to race or tries to control your experience, ask God for the grace to be still, making space for Him to speak His peace into your heart. Be aware of what you are feeling.[43]

When your time has ended, thank the Lord for always holding you—for being a very big, exquisitely brilliant God—even when you are not in a hammock or reclining. Now go on with your day in peace.

RECORD: Describe how you felt during this exercise as you began to let your mind relax?

What, if anything, did Jesus say to you?

What pictures came to mind?

This week, ask God to help you slow your mind so you can be more receptive to Him, especially when you need to be still, relax, and let go.

---

[43] Thanks to my friend, Nancy McDowell, for sharing her meditative prayer model from which this activity is adapted.

Share about your experience with a friend you can trust, asking him to check in with you next month about how you are learning to slow your mind, let go, and relax with God.

Write a prayer, committing your steps to the Lord (see Psalm 37:5).

Week 3 ~ **The Intellectual** ~

INTEGRATION: Review the last two weeks. What has God been teaching you?

How will you be intentional in the days ahead to be sure you partner with God in the things He is teaching you?

If there are ways you need to take action in the future, write them here or in your journal.

Now receive God's total grace and reflect upon His unalterable love for you—no matter how you feel you did on these spiritual exercises the last few weeks.

7
The Naturalist
Loving God through Experiencing Him Outdoors

Intermediate Spiritual Practices for the Naturalist

Week 1 ~ **The Naturalist** ~

READ: For those with a Naturalist Spiritual Temperament, God's creation is like an icon pointing them to Him. They feel closest to the Lord when surrounded by nature, and their souls come alive in the out-of-doors: the mountains, deserts, woods, or at the ocean. It's as they are surrounded by God's natural splendor that they feel most spiritually refreshed and connected with God.

Since the beginning of recorded time, God has been meeting His people in the out-of-doors, namely, in a garden. From Eden (see Genesis 2) to Gethsemane, where Jesus retreated to be with His Father during His darkest hour (see Matthew 26), it was to a garden that God's people went to find communion with Him, and the "sacred space" they needed to be vulnerable with Abba. For Adam and Eve, it was in the garden that they walked and talked with God in the cool of the day; it was also the place where they failed their greatest test (see Genesis 3). Yet for Jesus, the garden was the setting where He gained victory over the suffering, separation, and sin-bearing that was to come, receiving the profound comfort and strength He needed to endure the Cross.[44]

REFLECT: Where do you most often find your "sacred space" with God, the place you receive the strength, comfort, and reassurance you need—especially during difficult times?

Why do you choose this place?

---

[44] Isn't God amazingly creative and precise to give us such beautiful parallelism in the garden?!

If this spot is not outdoors, how different would it be for you to meet God outside for prayer and communion with Him at least a few times each week?

RESPOND: This week, at the beginning of each day, find a garden-like spot—a quiet place outdoors—where you can be with the Father. As you meet together, allow Him to give you fresh perspective, strength, comfort, and His joy. Consider Jesus in Gethsemane, and ask the Lord to give you grace to surrender your will as Jesus did, trusting the ultimate outcome of your life into the hands of your all-knowing Father.

If there's not a place outdoors that you to go to find deep connection with the Lord, or if it's too hot, cold, noisy, crowded, dangerous, etc., to be outside, find a spot inside where you can see some of God's created beauty: maybe gazing out a window, looking at some flowers, or even viewing a land or seascape. Be with Abba in this place as many times as possible this week.

RECORD: How was your time with God different this week as you met in "your garden spot"?

In what ways did Jesus' garden experience in Gethsemane encourage you to surrender your circumstances and life more fully to Abba?

Share with a friend you can trust about your time this week meeting the Lord in nature; ask her to check in with you next month to see how your outdoors rendezvous with God are going.

Write a prayer, committing your steps to the Lord (see Psalm 37:5).

READ: God is the grand Creator, and because we are made us in His image, His creation often inspires creativity in us. We see that God's design is not simply functional, but He is a God of limitless variety, detail, and extravagant beauty. The French mystic, Simone Weil, once said, "The soul's natural inclination to love beauty is the trap God most frequently uses in order to win [our souls to Him]."

The loveliness of God's creation has the power to move us because His creation is still speaking—as it always has—of the wonder and magnificence of God (see Psalm 19:1-4). Beauty is not just a characteristic of what God makes; it's also a description of who God is. Perhaps nothing shouts more loudly about the lavishness of God's holiness, justice, mercy, kindness, and tender care than aspects of His natural creation. Consider these words, which were inspired by our Creator:

THE WILD CHRIST
I surrender to an infinite Christ,
not a local, owned version but a spontaneous sanity of silence
who makes the Pleiades burn in utterly pure flame;
who smears the orange chalk of the sun all over the leaves and bodies of the trees,
who rides careening clouds, like gray ponies prancing down wild rivers of wind,
who changes breezes into His angel to whisper a spacious laugh of liberty,
who puts a silver moistness in dark valleys,
a seep between mountains where the wild ones drink;
who cherishes birds passionately…
from the inside they have to sing!
who swells succulent grasses for the white teeth of cattle,
who breathes life into a sullen bear
and sucks it out again when those dark, simmering eyes cease to burn;
who makes pear trees drip slow, golden bodies for the juice of the sun;
who seduces water into wine in every grape of the world
to celebrate a perpetual wedding feast;
who makes the human heart like a candle in meditation
to spout through it words as sputters of flame in a wind—
to sing His own wonder at the infinite plentitude
of Wisdom's everywhere wise, spontaneous lush of being.
This is the wild Christ no one can tame!
This is the new, unknowable name.[45]

---

[45] Poem by Blake Steele, a mystic and a poet. Used with permission.

REFLECT: Where do you see the "Wild Christ" when you look at creation?

Some of us are creative when we use ink on paper to write poems, letters, books, journals, or prayers. Others of us create with crayons, paint, glue or clay; maybe it's in the kitchen, garage, or woodshop that our creativity blossoms. Or perhaps it's when we touch the piano, violin, drums, guitar, or trumpet that we craft our art. Some create beauty in their homes with furniture, flowers, silk, or taffeta. Whatever medium you enjoy, what would you make if you allowed yourself the luxury of being inspired by God, the creator, and His creation?

RESPOND: This week, as you allow creation to inspire you, ask the Lord to stir you to be creative in the way that best suits you. Perhaps you want to craft a poem, a song, or a story. Maybe you'll gather leaves or see colors that inspire you to redecorate a room in your home, adding color to your dining room table or office, or speaking out the loveliness you see in others. You may be inspired to visit a friend and bring flowers to her, or read her a children's book you know she'll enjoy. Allow God to move you through His creative genius, making time to wrap yourself in His beauty every day this week.

RECORD: Describe the ways your creativity was aroused this week?

What did you do this week that was fun, enlivening, and encouraging as you allowed God's handiwork to move you?

How does your soul feel more alive when you spend extended time luxuriating in the beauty of our original, artistic, imaginative God?

Share your experience with a friend you can trust, asking him to check in with you next month about how the Creator is inspiring *your* creativity to blossom.

Write a prayer, committing your steps to the Lord (see Psalm 37:5).

Week 3 ~ **The Naturalist** ~

INTEGRATION: Review the last two weeks. What has God been teaching you through His creation?

How will you incorporate what you are learning into your life on a regular basis?

If there are ways you need to take action in the future, write them here or in your journal.

Advanced Spiritual Practices for the Naturalist

Week 1 ~ **The Naturalist** ~

READ: God's creation teaches us about rhythms, timing, and the seasons of life and death. In our world, we often try to push and manipulate time to make things happen the way we want them to. But in God's creation, the seasons are required for a seed to flower or an egg to hatch, and when the flower has lost its petals or the chick has lost its breath, no amount of effort on our part can keep either of them alive. When we look at creation, we humans are put in our place, humbled by what we cannot control. Here we remember that we live on a planet effected by The Fall. We realize that we are not God, and even with all our technology and gadgets, we are not ultimately in charge. Droughts occur. Earthquakes happen. Snow falls, and nature never asks our permission to carry on. The earth doesn't check our schedules. The moon and sun and stars don't care what we have planned. Yet in all of this, we can find comfort in the One who is larger than we are—the Creator of all heaven and earth.

The prophet Isaiah articulated well the extent of God's immeasurable power and sovereign care when he said:

> "Who has measured the waters in the hollow of His hand, marked off the heavens with a [nine-inch] span, enclosed the dust of the earth in a measure, and weighed the mountains in scales and the hills in a balance? Who has directed the Spirit of the Lord, or as His counselor has taught Him? With whom did He take counsel, that instruction might be given Him? Who taught Him the path of justice and taught Him knowledge and showed Him the way of understanding? Behold, the nations are like a drop from a bucket and are counted as small dust on the scales; behold, He takes up the isles like a very little thing. And all Lebanon's [forests] cannot supply sufficient fuel, nor all its wild beasts furnish victims enough to burn sacrifices [worthy of the Lord].

"Have you not understood from the foundations of the earth? It is God Who sits above the circle (the horizon) of the earth, and its inhabitants are like grasshoppers; it is He Who stretches out the heavens like [gauze] curtains and spreads them out like a tent to dwell in, Who brings dignitaries to nothing, Who makes the judges and rulers of the earth as chaos (emptiness, falsity, and futility). Yes, these men are scarcely planted, scarcely are they sown, scarcely does their stock take root in the earth, when [the Lord] blows upon them and they wither, and the whirlwind or tempest takes them away like stubble. To whom then will you liken Me, that I should be equal to him? says the Holy One. Lift up your eyes on high and see! Who has created these? He Who brings out their host by number and calls them all by name; through the greatness of His might and because He is strong in power, not one is missing or lacks anything. Why, O Jacob, do you say, and declare, O Israel, "My way and my lot are hidden from the Lord, and my right is passed over without regard from my God?" Have you not known? Have you not heard? The everlasting God, the Lord, the Creator of the ends of the earth, does not faint or grow weary; there is no searching of His understanding. He gives power to the faint and weary, and to him who has no might He increases strength [causing it to multiply and making it to abound]. Even youths shall faint and be weary, and [selected] young men shall feebly stumble and fall exhausted. But those who wait for the Lord [who expect, look for, and hope in Him] shall change and renew their strength and power; they shall lift their wings and mount up [close to God] as eagles [mount up to the sun]; they shall run and not be weary, they shall walk and not faint or become tired" *(Isaiah 40:12-16, 21-31, Amplified Bible)*.

REFLECT: How do you experience powerlessness in the face of God's immense universe, especially those aspects of life that you cannot control?

When were there times that the rhythms of life and death forced you to yield, and how did you handle the truth that you cannot make things happen your way, at your time?

What in Scripture helps you trust God when you feel that you life is beyond your control?

RESPOND: Here or in your journal, list the things in your life that currently escape your management.

We know that God *can* change things in a moment, yet He has chosen to limit Himself by actually partnering with humankind, which means in part that He does not intervene in every event on planet earth. What would you like to see Him change, something or someone that is not responding to your wishes?

Consider, then record, how and why God's sovereign care might be allowing the current timing of this situation in a best case scenario:

What in the universe encourages you to trust God with those people and situations that you cannot move, change, or rearrange—especially at your preferred speed?

Write down the things in creation that remind you of God's unlimited capacity to partner with you in the details of your life (for example, the millions of galaxies of stars that God ordained, and the fact that He knows each one of them by name, see Psalm 8:3; 147:4).

Write a prayer of relinquishment, acknowledging your finite limitations and God's unlimited capacity to be trusted. Speak the truth that God is sovereign, that He sees and cares about every detail of your life; allow Him to comfort you as you confess afresh that He is bigger than your circumstances.

RECORD: How was it for you to ponder God's immensity as you practiced relinquishment this week?

What difference do you see in yourselves after consciously acknowledging your trust in an infinite God?

How did you sense Jesus' presence and peace as you were doing this exercise?

What needs to happen next?

Share your experience with a friend you can trust, asking her to check in with you next month about how you are living in the conscious awareness of an immense, good, all-knowing God.

Write a prayer now committing your steps to the Lord (see Psalm 37:5).

Week 2 ~ **The Naturalist** ~

READ: It is good to recall that the Lord is the Master over all the forces of nature, even the wind and the waves. We see this clearly in Jesus' interaction with nature when He was on the Lake of Galilee with His disciples:

> "Let's go over to the other side of the lake." And they launched out. But as they were sailing along He fell asleep; and a fierce gale of wind descended upon the lake, and they began to be swamped and to be in danger. And they came to Him and woke Him up, saying, "Master, Master, we are perishing!" And being aroused, He rebuked the wind and the surging waves, and they stopped, and it became calm. And He said to them, "Where is your faith?" And they were fearful and amazed, saying to one another, "Who then is this, that He commands even the winds and the water, and they obey Him" (*Luke 8:22-25*).

REFLECT: Imagine what it must have been like to be with Jesus and feel constantly unprepared—even jarred and unsettled—by His tendency to say and do the unexpected, even the supernatural. How do you think you would have responded in this same situation had you been with Jesus in the boat as it was filling with water?

As you reread the passage now, what strikes you about Jesus' character and behavior in this story?

The Scripture tells us that after Jesus fell asleep, a fierce gale of wind descended and the boat was actually in danger. The disciples were not over-reacting or making a mountain out of a molehill. The ship truly was filling with water! Perhaps this was not a typical storm; maybe the enemy brought it on, intending to wipe out the Son of God and His disciples. Why do you think Jesus was able to sleep during this severe storm?

If you had Jesus' perspective and knew what He knows, how might that now alter your peace in the storms you are currently facing?

Jesus' storm was real; the water in the boat was real; the danger of drowning was real! Why, then, do you think Jesus asked His disciples, "Where is your faith?"

What do you think He expected His disciples to do?

RESPOND: In the account of this storm, perhaps the Son of God was sleeping because He knew His Father wasn't. The Scriptures say,

> "My help comes from the Lord, the Maker of heaven and earth.
> He will not let your foot slip—he who watches over you will not slumber;
> indeed, He who watches over Israel will neither slumber nor sleep.
> The Lord watches over you—the Lord is your shade at your right hand;

the sun will not harm you by day, nor the moon by night.
The Lord will keep you from all harm—He will watch over your life;
the Lord will watch over your coming and going both now and
forevermore" *(Psalm 121:2-8).*

(Isn't it nice to know that Father God, the Sovereign, all-powerful One, is never
sleeping on the job?)

Do you think the disciples could have used their own faith and the authority of
Jesus to rebuke the wind and waves themselves by saying, "Peace, be still"? Why or
why not?

How do you think these words of Jesus might apply: "I tell you the truth, anyone
who has faith in me will do what I have been doing. He will do even greater things
than these, because I am going to the Father" (John 14:12)?

How might this truth allow you to use God's delegated authority to stop the
enemy's storms in your life—literally or otherwise?

Think about, then list here or in your journal, the areas in your life where God's
authority needs to be exercised over the enemy and the elements. Partner with
Jesus now in prayer and speak to the storms in your life, using your delegated
authority to say, "Peace, be still," to each one.

(Note: In my life, I have learned that God empowers me *[and expects me]* to use the authority He's given me to calm the *literal* storms around me! This first happened many years ago during a severe thunder and lightening storm when my little dog, Suzi, awakened me in the night by pressing her wet, trembling nose against my cheek. Because she had an acute fear of loud noises, the thunder had sent her to my bed terrified. As I awoke to see how frightened she was, without hesitation or fore-thought, the Galatians 5:6 type of "faith working through love" (NASB) arose in me, and I found myself speaking to the storm, "Peace, be still!" The words were barley out of my mouth when all the thunder and lightening stopped—instantly! Because this was the first time I'd ever seen something like this happen, I assumed it was a coincidence. I looked at the clock, logged the time in my mind, thanked the Lord, and went back to sleep. The next day some friends who lived in a town close by told me that they had been out in their backyard watching the same storm during the night, and at the same exact moment that I spoke those words, they witnessed all the rain, thunder, and lightening stopping—instantly!! They were baffled by what had caused this extravagant show of sights and sounds to instantaneously cease, and as they told me their experience, I realized the meaning of Jesus words when He said our faith in Him will allow us to do what He does. Jesus really does impart HIS faith and authority to us to stop the real-life storm around us—even today!)

RECORD: How did you partner with God this week over the enemy and the elements?

What new insights and initiatives did you sense God giving you as you prayed?

Share your insights with a friend you can trust, asking him to check in with you next month to see how you are learning to partner with Jesus and bring His peace into your life and the lives of others on a regular basis.

Write a prayer, committing your steps to the Lord (see Psalm 37:5).

Week 3 ~ The Naturalist ~

INTEGRATION: Review the last two weeks. What has God been teaching you?

How will you be intentional so that the things you are learning become a regular part of your life?

If there are ways you need to take action in the future, write them here or in your journal.

Now receive God's total grace and reflect upon His unalterable love for you—no matter how you feel you did on these spiritual exercises the last few weeks.

8

The Sensate
Loving God through the Senses

Intermediate Spiritual Practices for the Sensate

Week 1 ~ **The Sensate** *~*

READ: When people find themselves enjoying and even getting lost in the man-made beauty around them, especially in church—whether it's intricate architecture or stained glass—they may have a Sensate spiritual temperament. Sensates are often tactile, visual, and kinesthetic worshipers who express their love for God through their senses, including taking pleasure in the magnificence of choral and classical music.

Music must be extremely important to God, because it's mentioned in the Bible from Genesis to Revelation. Even at Creation, the Bible describes how the morning stars sang together and the angels lifted up their voices in joy (see Job 38:6-7). Here are a few examples of when heaven sang:

> "The angel said, 'Don't be afraid. I'm here to announce a great and joyful event that is meant for everybody, worldwide: a Savior has just been born in David's town, a Savior who is Messiah and Master.'. . . At once the angel was joined by a huge angelic choir singing God's praises" (*Luke 2:10-13, The Message*).

> "I heard a voice from heaven, like the sound of many waters and like the sound of loud thunder, and the voice which I heard was like the sound of harpists playing on their harps. And they sang a new song before the throne" (*Revelation 14:2-3, NASB*).

> "The Lord your God is living among you. He is a mighty savior. He will take delight in you with gladness. With his love, he will calm all your fears. He will rejoice over you with joyful songs" (*Zephaniah 3:17, NLT*).

REFLECT: Have you ever wondered what these events were (or will be) like?
  • the morning stars singing together and the sons of God shouting for joy;

• the angelic choir lighting up the sky and singing at Christ's birth;

• the throne of God with the elders and thousands of saints singing to the Lamb;

• the Lord Himself singing a happy song over you.

If you could experience only one of these events, which would you most like to see and hear, and why?

RESPOND: Select some music to listen to now, preferably classical or contemporary worship songs that have no words. You may want to listen to Handel's *Messiah* or Pachelbel's "Canon in D"; any soothing instrumental music will do. Then use your spirit-led imagination to listen for heaven's voice through the sound and mood of the music. Allow the melody to suggest words and a story as you listen. Let the song become a prayer, a melody of love between you and the Lord, and let your soul be "held" by the music as it unfolds.

RECORD: How did experiencing this music inspire your connection with God?

What did you learn about yourself and the Lord as you listened?

What surprised you?

What blessed you?

Share about your experience with a friend you can trust, asking her to check in with you next month to see how your life is expanding as you luxuriate with the God of music and song.

Write a prayer, committing your steps to the Lord (see Psalm 37:5).

Week 2 ~ **The Sensate** ~

READ: When Jesus walked the earth, He often spoke of the coming events as if they were already true; He even invited his disciples to believe and pray for the unseen in that way, instructing them, "Whatever you ask for in prayer, believe that you *have received it,* and it will be yours" *(Mark 11:24, emphasis added).*

In Hebrews, it is recorded, "Faith is being sure of what we hope for and certain of what *we do not see" (Hebrews 11:1, emphasis added).* As we partner with God in prayer, He allows us to use our God-given, God-surrendered imaginations to visualize the unseen by faith. In His grace, He then invites us to trust Him to call that which is not yet visible into being.

REFLECT: When you pray, do you usually visualize people and circumstances as they are now—their current condition? Or do you imagine people and things in your mind from the perspective of how they would be if God's "good, pleasing, and perfect will" was occurring in their lives (see Romans 12:2)?

How might your prayer life change if you prayed for people and circumstances from a heavenly perspective, calling into being what you are hoping for, and visualizing with God what you imagine He wants to happen?

As you intercede for others, how do you sense yourself partnering with the Almighty, knowing that He has given you authority to work with Him by asking boldly on others' behalf—believing that you have received that for which you're asking?

RESPOND: On a note card, write the names of 5-10 people you feel led to intercede for this week. Feel free to fill up the card with names if you'd like. These may be friends or family members, people coping with chronic illnesses, loved ones far away from the Lord, or just people for whom you want to pray.[46]

Now as you talk to God, look at each name on the card; visualize the face of the person for whom you are praying. Take a few moments to focus on him, seeing all the features you can remember. Picture his face as it might be at this moment. Then, as you think of that person, with his face still in your mind's eye, invite the Lord to lead you to His Kingdom purpose for them. See the Lord touching that person and providing exactly what you are asking. If you are praying for people who are ill, picture the Lord healing them. If you are praying for people who are not trusting Jesus, imagine their life fruitful for the Lord. Based on what God has led you to pray, speak aloud your requests. (If you are not sure how to begin, you may want to use words like these:

> Lord, I bring to You [name]; surround her with Your loving arms this day and give her great strength and courage.

> Lord, I lift up [name]; may Your healing hand touch him and raise him out of that place of sickness and depression, and fill her with health and joy).

Continue to pray as needed moving through your list by visualizing each person and each request. Write down the date and what you pictured for each person. Be ready to see God's answers when they come.[47]

RECORD: How did your prayer time change this week as you began to intercede for people through visualization?

---

[46] You might want to use a rolodex of pictures of family and friends like I do, and I pray for one or a dozen of them each day, I look at their pictures as I partner with God on their behalf.

[47] Exercise adapted from Floyd W. Churn, "Nourishment for Peculiar Pilgrims on the Journey of Faith," DMin. Dissertation, Princeton Theological Seminary, 1995, 119.

How was Jesus present with you as you talked with Him this week about those He loves and for whom He died?

What do you want to do next to keep your prayer life becoming even more relevant and powerful?

Share your experience with a friend you can trust, asking him to check in with you next month about how you are interceded for people through visualization, and any further action you need to take.

Write a prayer now committing your steps to the Lord (see Psalm 37:5).

Week 3 ~ **The Sensate** ~

INTEGRATION: Review the last two weeks. What has God taught you?

How will you integrate what you are learning into your life?

If there are ways you need to take action in the future, write them here or in your journal.

Advanced Spiritual Practices for the Sensate

Week 1 ~ **The Sensate** ~

READ: The art created by humankind can speak powerfully of God Himself: His Kingdom come, His eternal power, and His unsurpassed brilliance. Sometimes a masterpiece seen on canvas or expressed through stained glass leads us to an awareness of the Lord's magnificent works throughout history, fueling our devotion to Him. When we see God's character and attributes reflected in a painting, a sculpture, or some marvelous work of art, these visual depictions give concrete expression to God's vast and loving invent. And whether they are found in a museum of religious works (such as Michelangelo's portrayal of the creation of Adam), or a book of simple landscapes or illustrations of children at play, art can move us to an awareness of the immeasurable winsomeness of God.

This week, as you drive around your town, be aware of what catches your eye; it may be the architecture of a cathedral, a museum, or a High Church with icons or paintings. Then select a place of beauty you can go to for a morning or afternoon, somewhere that speaks to you of our great, eternal Designer and Architect—God. If you can't find a location that suits you, look for a painting, a statue, or a stained-glass window on which you can focus. Allow yourself time to sit and become absorbed in the message of the art and artist as it speaks to you. Study what humankind can do, and let it inspire you to praise our first and most original Artist.

RECORD: How did the beauty of art, architecture, statues, or stained glass inspire you spiritually this week?

What did you learn about the Lord?

What were you prompted to do as a result of focusing upon this piece of created beauty?

Share about your time with a friend you can trust, asking her to check in with you next month about how the created beauty around you is stirring you to love and worship God.

Write a prayer, committing your steps to the Lord (see Psalm 37:5).

Week 2 ~ **The Sensate** ~

READ: Even though worship goes beyond the singing of songs, one way to experience God's presence is through the use of prayer chants, a spiritual exercise going back to our Judeo-Christian roots. Just as gloves adapt themselves to hands, so chants adapt themselves to prayer, allowing prayer to become a window through which we gaze at God.

Chanting is a rhythmic, verbal and auditory practice. Likened to praying through song, a chant is different from a hymn because, while a hymn is linear—moving from a beginning to an end, usually through several verses—a chant is circular, relying upon repetition to facilitate the experience.[48] Long before a system of musical notation was developed, Jews and monks learned to chant orally, gathering a repertoire of more than five thousand melodies that are still chanted today. Psalm 136:1-5 (NASB) gives us an example of a biblical chant:

> *Give thanks to the LORD, for He is good,*
> For His loving-kindness is everlasting.
>
> Give thanks to the God of gods,
> For His loving-kindness is everlasting.
>
> Give thanks to the Lord of lords,
> For His loving-kindness is everlasting.
>
> To Him who alone does great wonders,
> For His loving-kindness is everlasting;

---

[48] Floyd W. Churn, "Nourishment for Peculiar Pilgrims on the Journey of Faith," 132.

To Him who made the heavens with skill,
For His loving-kindness is everlasting.

REFLECT: How familiar are you with Christian chanting?

In what context have you seen, heard, or experienced this (if you saw the movie, "The Sound of Music", the opening scene shows nuns reciting a musical chant in Latin)?

If Christian chanting is new to you, think about how God has met you in the past through new and unfamiliar experiences. Invite the Lord to meet you again as you enjoy this fresh experience of worshipping Him through a chant.

RESPOND: Begin to worship with a prayer chant by using the repetitive phrase in Psalm 136, "His loving-kindness is everlasting." As you begin, think of ways you have experienced the Lord's loving-kindness in the last few months. Then spontaneously create words of praise or thanksgiving you can chant. Sing the words by keeping them on one note, with the exception of the next to the last syllable, which is raised or lowered by a third. In the word "ever-lasting," the syllable "last" will be lowered a third. This gives the chant a harmonic, dissonant flavor. (If you have heard Gregorian chants or the psalms sung in a monastery, this process may be quite familiar to you.)

The important thing is not that you sing the notes of the chant correctly, but that you pray aloud to the Lord in a way that makes His goodness more vivid in your heart and mind. Don't worry about the tune; just make one up if that suits you better, or use my suggested breaks here:

Thank You, Lord, for help-ing me get this pro-ject com-plet-ed (hold the last note),
Your lov-ing-kind-ness is e-ver-la-a-sting.

I love You, Lord, for the grace and en-er-gy You give me,
Your lov-ing-kind-ness is e-ver-la-a-sting.

May You re-ceive glor-y and plea-sure from my life, Lord,
Your lov-ing-kind-ness is e-ver-la-a-sting.

Now put in your own words, and let them be spontaneous, ending each impromptu phrase with, "Your loving-kindness is everlasting."

Engage this exercise all week long, using a different Psalm each time, or making up words of your own.

RECORD: How was your experience of singing prayer chants to the Lord this week?

Were you able to allow the Spirit to lead you through unfamiliar times of worship as you formed impromptu words of praise to God?

What did you learn about the Lord through chanting?

Share about your experience with a friend you can trust, asking her to check in with you next month about your ongoing life of prayer chanting to God.

Write a prayer, committing your steps to the Lord (see Psalm 37:5).

Week 3 ~ **The Sensate** ~

INTEGRATION: Review the last two weeks. What has God been teaching you?

How will you continue to apply what you have learned?

If there are ways you need to take action in the future, write them here or in your journal.

Now receive God's total grace and reflect upon His unalterable love for you—no matter how you feel you did on these spiritual exercises the last few weeks.

9

The Traditionalist
Loving God through Ritual and Symbol

Intermediate Spiritual Practices for the Traditionalist

Week 1 ~ The Traditionalist ~

READ: For most of us, life is so variable and beyond our ability to manage that we find it necessary to establish rituals that keep life ordered and in rhythm. Just like the habit of brushing our teeth daily helps us care for our teeth, so spiritual habits help us care for our relationship with God. These rituals become spiritual practices that assist us as we enter into the majesty of a magnificent God whose glory is often "too great for human experience." [49]

The Bible teaches us to draw near to God with a heart that's prepared and ready to worship Him completely:

> "Give to the Lord the glory He deserves! Bring your offering and
> come into His presence. Worship the Lord in all His holy splendor"
> *(1 Chronicles 16:29, NLT).*

Here we are told to three things to do as we come to God:
1. Give the Lord the credit that already belongs to Him by recognizing with *reverent respect* who He is and all He has done. This means that we come with our souls clothed in humility, wonder, and trust.
2. Then we *sacrificially surrender* everything to Him, bringing ourselves as an offering, along with a gift—a present that costs us something.
3. And as we *worship and adore Him*, we pay special attention to His holiness, radiance, and magnificent worth, which is the core of worship.

For the person with a Traditionalist spiritual temperament, this heart-posture is the only suitable way to come to a holy God.

REFLECT: When we worship the Lord, sometimes we come expecting to get a blessing from Him. Other times we may come out of a sense of duty, need,

---

[49] Gary Thomas, *Sacred Pathways* (Nashville: Thomas Nelson, 1982), 88.

guilt, repentance, or even desperation. When you come to worship the Lord, what is most often the attitude of your heart?

What helps you become *reverently respectful* when you worship, mindful of who God is and all He has done, attentive to His nature and the glory He deserves?

How can you *sacrificially surrender* your life to the Lord so that you "constantly and at all times offer up to God a sacrifice of praise, which is the fruit of lips that thankfully acknowledge and confess and glorify His name" *(Hebrews 13:15, Amplified)*?

When you spend time *worshiping and adoring* God, how prepared and expectant are you to experience His splendor and glory?

How do you attend to His holiness, radiance, and magnificent worth?

RESPOND: This week make time to come to God alone, giving Him your full attention. Begin in silence, allowing time to recall and meditate on who God is: His nature, His attributes, His love, kindness, goodness, faithfulness, gentleness, sovereign care, and holiness. Remember that He is all-knowing, everywhere present, all-powerful, and changeless, the eternal Creator, the Wonderful Counselor, Everlasting Father, Prince of Peace, King of Kings and Lord of Lords.

Then begin to remember His deeds throughout history, the acts miracles recorded in His Word throughout time (see Psalm 77:11). At this point, come near to Him as if entering His "gates" with thanksgiving, and coming into His "courts" with praise for all He has done for *you*: His faithfulness *to you*, His goodness, mercy, forgiveness, blessing, favor, direction, and how He's changed *your mourning* into dancing (see Psalm 100:4, Psalm 30:11).

Now bring the Lord an offering: a gift to further demonstrate your humble love. Begin by offering yourself to Him, making a decisive dedication of your body "[presenting all your members and faculties] as a living sacrifice, holy (devoted, consecrated) and well pleasing to God, which is your reasonable (rational, intelligent) service and spiritual worship" *(Romans 12:1, Amplified)*. This involves taking "your everyday, ordinary life—your sleeping, eating, going-to-work, and walking-around life—and [placing] it before God as an offering. Embracing what God does for you is the best thing you can do for Him" *(Romans 12:1, The Message)*.

Be sure you bring an offering to Him that costs you something; it may be in the form of money given to someone who is doing God's work; it could be a tithe to your church (if you are not already doing that). It may be something sacrificial you do for a person in need, a deed you keep secret between with the Lord. It may be your commitment to fast, asking God to increase your hunger for Him, or letting go of any resistance to lifting your hands in surrender and praise in the congregation (or when you are worshipping God alone). Your sacrifice may be your willingness to dance before the Lord in the privacy of your own home, even though that is not comfortable for you or an expression you would normally choose. Ask God to show you what sacrifice of praise He would like from you (remembering, of course, you can't out-give God!).

End your time in silent worship, resting in the presence of God's holiness, radiance, and magnificent worth.

RECORD: How was your experience of worshipping the Lord this week?

How did you experience the Lord's presence as you were *reverently and respectfully* mindful of who He is and all He has done, attentive to the glory He deserves?

In what ways did you *sacrificially surrender* yourself, bringing Him an offering of praise, something that was valuable to you?

As you *worshiped and adored Him,* how did you pay special attention to His holiness, radiance, and magnificent worth?

What steps do you still need to take?

Share your experience with a friend you can trust, asking him to check in with you next month about how your times of heart preparation are going as you worship God.

Write a prayer now committing your steps to the Lord (see Psalm 37:5).

Week 2 ~ **The Traditionalist** ~

READ: In the Bible, many of God's people built altars to represent victories or special times when the Lord's presence "altered" their lives in significant ways (such as Noah in Genesis 8:20; Abraham in Genesis 12:7; Isaac in Genesis 26:25; Jacob in Genesis 35:1,7; Moses in Exodus 17:15; and Joshua in Joshua 8:30).

God instructed His people to build an altar of remembrance after encounters with Him; then each generation was to teach the next generation how to build an altar of stones as a memorials to God as well. We see this happening when the Amalekites attacked Israel at Rephidim: the Israelites won the battle because Joshua and his men fought with the sword and Moses held up the staff of God in his hands (with Aaron and Hur supporting him—one on either side— keeping his hands steady from sunrise till sunset). When the battle ended, God told Moses to write about this on a scroll as "something to be remembered and make sure that Joshua hears it. . . . Moses then built an altar and called it The Lord is my Banner'" (*Exodus 17:14-15*); this altar symbolized the victory Israel attained in partnership with the Living God.

REFLECT: Consider all the times God has led you and met you in significant ways: giving you His divine strategies, sending you friends to fight along side you, support you, hold you steady, and partner with you while God did His 100% (the part you can't do), and you do your 100% (the part you can do). Write some of these times here or in your journal:

If you were to build an altar of stones representing the times when God "altered" your circumstances, what would your stones signify?

RESPOND: With your family or close friends (those who've supported you in the spiritual victories you've won), construct an altar to the Lord. Gather in a significant place in your yard, a nearby park, by a river, on a mountain top, or somewhere you can build a small altar that you will be able to visit later as you recall God's work in your life. Begin by collecting actual stones—five to ten for each person—with more available as needed. Find enough rocks so that all who gather can signify on her stones what the Lord has done, remembering the special times He has led and blessed you, both individually and as a family or group. Do not minimize this experience for children, even though you may need to help them remember times when God answered their prayers and blessed them.

Allow everyone time to remember God's work, writing on the stones with a permanent marker the title or theme of the event, and/or words of praise for the victory. When everyone is finished writing, begin to build the altar. It may be good to go around the circle, allowing each person to share and then place on the altar one stone at a time. (If you live where constructing an altar of stone is not feasible, consider drawing an altar in your journal or using paper stones to make a collage.)

Once your altar is built, give people an opportunity to share about its overall meaning to them. Close your time in prayer, inviting everyone who would like to express their thanks to God for His faithfulness.

Revisit your altar often, remembering all the things God has done for you—individually, as a family, or as a group of believers.

RECORD: How did your family or friends respond to building an altar together?

What did you learn about the Lord?

What did you learn about your family or friends?

How did you experience the Lord's presence with you while you did this exercise?

What follow-up do you need to do now?

Share your experience with a friend you can trust, asking her to check in with you next month to see how building and revisiting your alter is going.

Write a prayer now committing your steps to the Lord (see Psalm 37:5).

Week 3 ~ **The Traditionalist** ~

INTEGRATION: Review the last two weeks. What has God been teaching you?

How will you integrate what you have learned into your life?

If there are ways you need to take action in the future, write them here or in your journal.

Advanced Spiritual Practices for the Traditionalist

Week 1 ~ **The Traditionalist** ~

READ: Change is unavoidable. Things wear out and new items must be purchased or built to replace the old. Jobs come and go; friends and family move or pass away. We age. In this life, nothing remains the same—except God who is permanently constant and unalterable! Thankfully, "Jesus Christ is the same yesterday and today and forever" (*Hebrews 13:8*).

For all of us, change can be uncomfortable. Yet for the Traditionalist, alterations can be seen as undermining the timelessness of the faith. Because Traditionalists feel connected to God when they worship Him as they have before, repetition aids them in accessing a vast, mysterious God. And when this is taken away, embracing change becomes the Traditionalist's growing edge— even when God Himself is initiating something new.

REFLECT: As you look back, consider all the changes in your life, both those that have been helpful and those that were particularly hard. Write two or three of the major changes here or in your journal:

Think through the life of Jesus. Consider all the changes He ushered in, and how many of the religious people of His day resisted those changes. Write some of the changes His life brought to the people of His day and for all time:

Are there changes occurring in your life (or in your church), alterations you are watching take place around you, ones you may be resisting? If so, what comes to mind?

Consider each change, and ponder how Jesus may actually be ushering you into these new places. If you are passively looking on or actively resisting, how might the Lord be inviting you to cooperate more fully with Him?

RESPOND: Go through the book of Acts in the New Testament this week. Record all the changes God brought to His people—first-time experiences for His church:

In what ways did the people of that day respond to these changes, both positively and negatively?

How would you have handled the Spirit's movement if God had brought so many changes to your life or church that quickly?

When you look at your life, how might God be inviting you to respond the same way or differently than those in the early church?

RECORD: What did God show you about Himself this week?

What did you realize about yourself and the changes happening around you?

Ask your spouse or a close friend to pray with you, inviting God to give you the grace to accept His changes with peace and trust in your unchanging God.

Share your insights with a friend you can trust, asking him to check in with you next month about how you are handling these changes.

Write a prayer, committing your steps to the Lord (see Psalm 37:5).

READ: In the Bible, we are given instructions about what to do with our minds and the eyes of our hearts. Perhaps this is because God knows we have a tendency to look around us and worry or fret, forgetting who He is—and who we are in Him. Here is what He says:

> "You will keep in perfect peace all who trust in You, all whose thoughts are fixed on you!" *(Isaiah 26:3, NLT)*.

> "Let us fix our eyes on Jesus, the author and perfecter of our faith, who for the joy set before him endured the cross, scorning its shame, and sat down at the right hand of the throne of God" *(Hebrews 12:2)*.

> "So we fix our eyes not on what is seen, but on what is unseen. For what is seen is temporary, but what is unseen is eternal" *(2 Corinthians 4:18)*.

Jesus, too, asks us to remember Him and what He did for us when we gather. He gave us this sacrament and command: "He took bread, gave thanks and broke it, and gave it to them, saying, 'This is my body given for you; do this in remembrance of me'" *(Luke 22:19)*.

The Lord instituted times for us to remember Him together; this includes focusing on His great sacrifice for us, as well as who we are to Him as those He loves us enough to suffer and die on the cross so we could be with Him forever.

And as we remember *Him*, so He is remembering *us*. As we are drinking the cup, He is refraining from drinking the cup until we are with Him in His Kingdom: "Mark my words—I will not drink wine again until the day I drink it new with you in my Father's Kingdom" *(Matthew 26:29, NLT)*.

Remembering is so important. It keeps our minds focused on the truth, that this earth is not our home; in fact, we are aliens and strangers here (see Hebrews 11:13). We are passing through this temporary dwelling, and we will spend eternity with our Lord… feasting with Him in our permanent, heavenly home. That is certainly worth remembering!

REFLECT: Consider how you take time to remember Jesus, what He has done for you, and that He is waiting for *you* to join Him at His banqueting table. Do you set aside time to do this daily, weekly, or monthly? Why or why not?

How are you using the Communion table (the bread and wine, symbolizing the body and blood of Christ) to recall and meditate upon Jesus?

In what ways can you increase your awareness of what Jesus did and is doing for you, as well as the fact that He is awaiting the moment you will join Him in His Kingdom at the marriage supper of the Lamb (see Revelation 19:9)?

RESPOND: This week, take the Communion elements often—the bread and wine (or grape juice)—as a reminder of the Lord's sacrifice, then and now. If you feel more comfortable doing this in a liturgical setting, find a priest who will serve you (and anyone in your home who'd also like to participate). If you feel at ease taking Communion in your home, feel free to take the elements there—alone or with those in your family who would like to join you.

Begin by preparing some bread and wine (or grape juice). Then read this Scripture:

> "I received from the Lord that which I also delivered to you, that the Lord Jesus in the night in which He was betrayed took bread; and when He had given thanks, He broke it and said, 'This is My body, which is for you; do this in remembrance of Me.' In the same way He took the cup also after supper, saying, 'This cup is the new covenant in My blood; do this, as often as you drink it, in remembrance of Me.' For as often as you eat this bread and drink the cup, you proclaim the Lord's death until He comes" (*1 Corinthians 11:23-26, NASB*).

As you take the bread, break it and say, "This is the body of Christ, which was broken for us." Now eat the bread slowly, remembering Christ's body broken for you. (If you are taking Communion with another person, give the bread to one another, saying, "This is the body of Christ, which was broken for you.") Don't rush through this; take a few moments to just ponder the meaning.

Then drink the wine or grape juice and say, "This is the blood of Christ, poured out for my sins and the sin of the whole world." Drink it slowly, remembering Christ's blood shed for you. (If you are taking Communion with another person, give the wine or grape juice to one another saying, "This is the blood of Christ, which was spilled for you.")

Now talk to Jesus, thanking Him for His broken body, His suffering, His sacrifice and surrender to the Father, His cleansing blood that pours over you leaving you spotless, white as snow in the Father's eyes (see Isaiah 1:18).

After you are done, do as Jesus did and sing a hymn or one of your favorite worship songs (see Matthew 26:30).

RECORD: How were your times of Communion this week?

How did remembering Jesus bring you closer to Him?

What did you learn about the Lord?

Share your experience with a friend you can trust, asking her to check in with you next month about how taking Communion has helped you remember the One who always remembers you.

Write a prayer, committing your steps to the Lord (see Psalm 37:5).

Week 3 ~ **The Traditionalist** ~

INTEGRATION: Review the last two weeks. What has God been teaching you?

How will you make what you have learned a regular part of your life?

If there are ways you need to take action in the future, write them here or in your journal.

Now receive God's total grace and reflect upon His unalterable love for you—no matter how you feel you did on these spiritual exercises the last few weeks.

About the Author

Dr. Myra Perrine has a passion for intimacy with God, and has been speaking and teaching on this subject for more than four decades. She holds a Doctor of Ministry in Spiritual Formation, and a Master's of Arts in Education and Counseling. Working with Church Resource Ministries (CRM) since 1995, Myra coaches leaders around the world. As the founder of *The 3D Network*, she helps people discover how they were *Designed by* God to *Dream with* God and step into their *Destiny in* God. Having traveled and taught in over 45 nations, Myra is an adjunct professor at Simpson University and A. W. Tozer Theological Seminary. She and her husband, Dan, live in Redding, California, where they enjoy boating, kayaking, having dinner with friends, and traveling with their dogs. They have one grown son, three "adopted" daughters, and six "adopted" grandchildren.

Other books written by Dr. Perrine are:
What's Your God Language?
Connecting with God Through Your Unique Spiritual Temperament,

What's Your God Language? Coaching Guide,

Becoming One: Nurturing Spiritual Intimacy in Marriage,

Touching the Hem of His Garment: A Guide for Encountering God

Made in the USA
Charleston, SC
14 October 2015